HONOUR TRIUMPHANT;

AND

A LINE OF LIFE:

TWO TRACTS BY

JOHN FORDE, THE DRAMATIST,

UNKNOWN TO THE EDITORS OF HIS WORKS,

AND

NOW FIRST REPRINTED FROM THE ORIGINAL COPIES

PUBLISHED IN

1606 AND 1620.

LONDON:

PRINTED FOR THE SHAKESPEARE SOCIETY.

———

1843.

LONDON:
F. SHOBERL, JUN., 51, RUPERT STREET, HAYMARKET,
PRINTER TO H.R.H. PRINCE ALBERT.

COUNCIL

OF

THE SHAKESPEARE SOCIETY.

President.

THE MOST NOBLE THE MARQUESS OF CONYNGHAM.

Vice-Presidents.

RT. HON. LORD BRAYBROOKE, F.S.A.

RT. HON. LORD FRANCIS EGERTON, M.P.

RT. HON. THE EARL OF GLENGALL.

RT. HON. EARL HOWE.

RT. HON. LORD LEIGH.

RT. HON. THE EARL OF POWIS.

AMYOT, THOMAS, ESQ., F.R.S., TREAS. S.A.

AYRTON, WILLIAM, ESQ., F.R.S., F.S.A.

BOTFIELD, BERIAH, ESQ., M.P., F.R.S., F.S.A.

BRUCE, JOHN, ESQ., F.S.A.

CLERKE, MAJOR T. H. SHADWELL, K.H., F.R.S.

COLLIER, J. PAYNE, ESQ., F.S.A., DIRECTOR.

COOPER, C. PURTON, ESQ., Q.C., F.R.S., F.S.A.

CORNEY, BOLTON, ESQ.

CUNNINGHAM, PETER, ESQ., TREASURER.

DICKENS, CHARLES, ESQ.

DYCE, REV. ALEXANDER.

FIELD, BARRON, ESQ.

HALLAM, HENRY, ESQ., F.R.S., V.P.S.A.

HALLIWELL, J. O., ESQ., F.R.S., F.S.A.

PETTIGREW, T. J., ESQ., F.R.S. F.S.A.

PLANCHÉ, J. R., ESQ., F.S.A.

SHARPE, THE REV. LANCELOT, M.A., F.S.A.

THOMS, WILLIAM J., ESQ., F.S.A.

TOMLINS, F. GUEST, ESQ., SECRETARY.

WATSON, SIR FREDERICK BEILBY, K.C.H., F.R.S.

WRIGHT, THOMAS, ESQ., M.A., F.S.A.

INTRODUCTION.

The two following tracts are by the celebrated dramatist, and contemporary of Shakespeare, John Forde, whose works have gone through two modern impressions, besides the ancient editions. The first tract is altogether unknown, and has escaped the researches of every literary antiquary : the last is mentioned in the Stationers' Register, under the date of October 10, 1620; and the late Mr. Gifford, (Ford's Works, i., xiii,) presumed that it was a lost play. The reader will find that it has nothing dramatic in its form, subject, or composition; but, as the production of so distinguished a stage-poet, and as it importantly illustrates the life and character of its author, independently of any literary claims, it was clearly worthy of preservation, and no apology can be necessary for reprinting it from the sole existing copy.

Mr. Gifford also mistakenly terms Luke Hutton's "Black Dog of Newgate" a play. That there was a drama with this title cannot be doubted : it is mentioned in Henslowe's Diary as the authorship of R. Hathway; but Hutton's tract is quite of a different character, being an attack, in prose and verse, chiefly upon the vices prevalent in London. The supposed author was hanged at York in 1598 for robbery, so that " The Black Dog of Newgate" must have appeared about that date; and we may presume that it was not penned by Hutton, but by some pamphleteer of the time, who wished to take advantage of the highwayman's notoriety. It was reprinted in 1638, with various changes and some additions, in order to give the work the appearance of novelty. An account of this impression is inserted in the " Bridgewater Catalogue," 4to, 1837, p. 149, and a copy of the original edition is in the British Museum.

" Honour Triumphant, or the Peer's Challenge, by Arms defensible, at Tilt, Turney, and Barriers," bears the date of 1606, and it was written in consequence of the royal celebrations on the arrival of the King of Denmark in London on the 17th July in that year: it must have been penned and printed with great speed, as his Danish majesty did not remain in England quite a month, having taken his departure, according to Camden, on the 14th August.

Forde was at this date not twenty-one, having been born in April, 1586: " Honour Triumphant " preceded his " Fame's Memorial," on the death of the Earl of Devonshire in 1606, so that we are entitled to consider it Forde's earliest work. It consists of four essays, or, more properly, orations, in support of four positions of chivalry, and the eloquent prose is intermixed with poetry. At the end are separate poems in honour of the Christian IV., obviously hasty efforts, intended perhaps to gratify the ear of James I., and to secure patronage to the author, who had been admitted a student of Gray's Inn in 1602.

His object in writing his "Line of Life," fourteen years afterwards, is not very evident; since it is of a much graver character than might be looked for from the author of the plays Forde had then unquestionably produced. It is written in a high moral tone; and the characters, inserted in the course of it, of the Earl of Essex, beheaded by Queen Elizabeth, and of Sir Walter Raleigh, executed by James I. so short a time before the tract was published, are very remarkable. It concludes with a flattering tribute to the king.

It may be right to add that "Honour Triumphant" was published in 4to, and the "Line of Life" in 12mo.

In order to render all that relates to so distinguished an author complete, we have added on the next page some commendatory poems upon Forde and his "Fame's Memorial:" they are omitted by Mr. Gifford, because perhaps, as they are on a separate leaf, the copy he used of this very rare production did not contain them. They are in themselves of little worth.

To Master John Forde, of the Middle Temple, upon his *Fames Memorial*, this Madrigal.

If that renowmed Lord (whose powerfull fame
  In strength of warres, and calmes of peace exceeded)
Hath after death purchas'd so great a name,
  That it must prosper as it hath proceeded ;
  Then must in time those spightful plants be weeded,
Which living, yet him living would have choaked ;
  And those sweet wittes, touch'd with the sacred flame
Of his rich virtues, shall advance the same.
But thou (by those deserts in him provoked)
  That song his honours which so much exceeded,
Whose pleasant pen, in sacred water soaked
  Of Castaly, did register his worth,
Reapest much part of honour for thy pen
Through him, faire mirror of our Englishmen,
  Whom with due dignity thy Muse set forth.

BAR. BARNES.

IN EUNDEM.

Vivit, in æternum vivet Dux inclitus armis,
  Mountjoyus : vivet, Forde, poema tuum,
Major uterque suo genio. Vi carminis heros,
  Materiæ fælix nobilis autor ope.

T. P.

HONOR

TRIVMPHANT:

OR

THE PEERES CHALLENGE,

by Armes defensible, at
Tilt, Turney, and Barriers.

In honor of all faire Ladies, and in defence of
these foure positions following.

1 *Knights in Ladies service haue no free-will.*
2 *Beauty is the mainteiner of valour.*
3 *Faire Lady was neuer false.*
4 *Perfect lovers are onely wise.*

Mainteined by Arguments.

ALSO

THE MONARCHES MEETING :

OR

The King of Denmarkes *welcome* into
England.

Tam Mercurio, quam Marti.

AT LONDON
Printed for Francis Burton.
1606.

To the most noble Lord, the Duke of *Lennox*
his Grace.

FIRST POSITION.

*Knights in Ladies service haue no
free-will.*

To the Right Honorable, the Earle of
Arundel.

SECOND POSITION.

Beauty is the mainteiner of valour.

To the Right Honorable, the Earle of
Pembrooke.

THIRD POSITION.

Faire Ladie was neuer false.

To the Right Honorable, the Earle of
Mountgomery.

FOURTH POSITION.

Perfect lovers are onely wise.

To the Rightly Honourable, and *truely worthy Ladies, the Countesse* of *Pembrooke,* and the Countesse of *Mountgomerie.*

Most Excellent Ladies.   Where perfect honour is ennobled with accomplisht perfection, beauty is not scant, which euermore is the glorious shrine of honourable favour ; else had I misconceited mine owne hopes, and beene gravelled in mine owne conceipts ; but my strong confidence is my confident warrant : neither can ye distust that which explanes but what is done for you, what is done by yours.   If the pleasure ye shall take in the Defenders, who are yours, by the defence which is for you, be great, then the acceptance cannot be lesse in reading the reasons for that defence, especially being to you devoted, and onely to you devoted.   What defects and weakly mainteyning arguments in the arguments there are, your protection shal wipe off, and the trueth it selfe (which needes no lustre) chiefly privilege.   I affect no singularity, I boast no affectation ; yet, can I not freeze in the one, when I am temperately heated with the other.   To whom (noble Countesses) should I dedicate the ornaments of love and beauty but to the beautifullest ornaments worthy to be beloved ?   Neither doubt I, but as these endeavours were willingly intended, so will they as gratefully bee accepted.   Otherwise (as I hope, as I feare not) I will be an alien to mine own issue, as unworthy to be christened for mine, since dis-esteemed in being mine.   Others who oppose themselves, if not by Mercury perswaded, I referre to be by Mars enforced.   So, adventuring at once all my deserts in your like or dislike, I rest,

Devoted to your honourable virtues,

JOHN FORDE.

TO EUERY SUNDRY OPINIONED READER.

I intend not to make any tedious apologie. If thou be my
friend, thou wilt censure friendly ; if a stranger, indifferently ;
if an enemie, I esteeme thee not. Then thus :——

> I write not to content each cavelling braine,
>   But eyes of noblest spirits : he that loues mee
> Will thanke my labours, and commend my veyne ;
>   For any others enuy, least it moues mee.
> He that will storme at euery wrongfull hate
> Must not referre it to desert, but fate.

> Let ladies smile opon my lines, I care not
>   For idle faults in graver censor's eye ;
> On whose opinion (truth it is) I dare not
>   The merit of my studies to rely :
> Heere is the comfort which doth cheere despaire ;
> I shall be likt not of the grave, but faire.

Meritum rependant venustæ.

HONOR TRYUMPHANT.

To the Right Noble Lord, the Duke of Lennox his Grace.

FIRST POSITION.
Knights in Ladies seruice haue no free-will.

RIGHT NOBLE LORD.

How certaine it is, both by the tradition of ancient and moderne judgements avowed, that euerie man is not borne for himselfe. The communication of the sawe, and the authoritie of reason, shall bee a priuiledge sufficient; but how much mistaken both the philosophers of old and later neotorickes haue been, their owne ignorance makes manifest. A man (say they) is partly borne for his countrey, partly for his parents, partly for his friends; nothing, or (if any thing yet) least and lastly for himselfe. True; yet had the sensible touch of passion toucht them with the feeling of a passionate sence, how much more, and more truely, might they haue affirmed, that the chiefest creation of man was (next his owne soule) to doe homage to the excellent frame of beautie—a woman : a woman, the art of nature, the liuely perfection of Heauen's architecture ! for though

Man be the little world where wonder lyes,

yet,

Women are saints aboue earth's paradise.

For what is he who is so absolute a lord of himselfe, so power-full in his owne power, so free of his owne affections, as being

ensnared in the pleasing seruitude of a gracious beautie, can, or
durst to undertake any occasion of remisnesse, but his own
hart will be the first guilty accuser of his owne folly, and his
sincere repentance doe pennance in the language of griefe, in
the griefe of despair? Againe, what is he, then, that, being free
from this captived happinesse of loue, as it were, disdaining to
stoope to the bondage of beautie, will not at length feel the
miserie of his scorne, and be scorned in the wracke of his
miserie? Besides, may hee not be desperate of his owne merit
to thinke himself the onely exiled abject, banished from out the
acceptance of a ladie's fauor, as also his owne vnworthinesse,
which cannot deserve so delicious a blessing? Say, then, such a
one be entertained as a happie seruant to a more glorious mistresse, how soone, how much is his owne free rule of himselfe
endeered to the commaund of a precious goddesse? neither then
hath he, neither is it mee the should haue, any more domination
ouer his owne affections. Mars throwes downe his weapons,
and Venus leads him captiue; the lustre of her eyes, and the
glorie of her worth, are of such vnresistable a force, as the
weaknesse of his manhood, or the aptnesse of his frailtie are
neither able to eudure the one's reflection, or withstand the
other's temptation. How then? must he yeeld? true; not to
captivitie, but freedome; for to bee captived to beautie is to
bee free to vertue. Who would not put of an armour of hard
steele, and turne from his enemies, to be enchained in pleasure,
and turne to a lady in a bed of soft down? Foolish hardinesse
is hardened foolishnesse, when securest loue is the loueliest
securitie.

Loue once was free from loue, and had a will
    To play the wanton wag: he strooke full many,
And tooke delight soft thought of ease to kill;
    Yet he himselfe was neuer spoyld of any.
Loue carelesse would go walke, when by a groue
Loue saw a nymph, when straight Loue fell in loue.

Cupid with Psiches fell in loue, whose beauty
  Dazled the lustre of his wandring eye;
Forcing his heart devote obsequious duty
  Vnto the wonder of her deity:
Herein was Cupid blind, who els could see
Loue now captiv'd his heart, which earst was free.

Loue hath no power ere he gaine his rest,
But to impawne, sweare, promise, and protest:
Alas! what is it, then, that men in bed
Will not vow, urge, to gain a maiden head;
Which, being got, they euer after stand
Devoted to their ladies' deere commaund?

Then, what man of reason is he, who would be so unreasonable in his owne desires, to wish himselfe obstinately foolish, or thinke himselfe foolishlie wise, by containing his owne dissolute infranchisment in the boundlesse limitts of his owne frantick wilfulnesse? Such, and of such nature are they, who, in the rancorous spleenes of an unpreuailing rancour, durst not onelie in the mallice of their tongues to speake, but in the venome of their hearts, to copy out whole pamphlets against the dignitie of the female sex; either without respect that they themselues came from a woman, or without regard that a woman wrought the peace for their weak-ballac't soules (oh, but say such): had not a woman beene the tempter and efficient of our fall, we had not needed a redemption. Alas! sillie betrayers of youre owne follie! wretched blasphemers against the perfection of nature! can ye not, or will yee not understand that the blessing of this fall is saluation? assurance of heauen? certainty of ioyes? Yes; it is doubtlesly probable that women are Nature's pride, Vertue's ornaments, Angels on earth worthy to be serued, saints in heauen memorable to be registred.

    Ne ii sunt amore digni,
    Quos indignos rejicit amor.

Would any man liue happie in content of mind? fortunate
in prosperitie of content? singular in the repute of account?
blessed in being inriched with earthe's rarest blessing? let him
then ennoble his deserts, by deseruing to be beloued: of whome?
of popular opinion, or unstable vulgar dependances? No ; but
of loue it selfe — a woman. Would any be miserable? let him
be excluded from the favour of beauty, and it is a misery incomparable, a torment vnspeakeable, a death, yea, a hell in-
sufferable. How, then, comes it to passe that some vaine op-
pugners of loue thinke, that, by seruing of a ladie, they themselues both honour in their loue, and ought to be honoured for
louing of their beloued? It is easily answered : by the imper-
fection of their manhood, and pride of their grosse, erronious
folly. For this, in the rules of affection, is text : whosoeuer
truely loue, and are truly of their ladies beloued, ought in their
service to employ their endeuours ; more for the honour and
deseruing the continuance of their ladies good-will, than any
way to respect the free-will of their owne heedlesse dispositions ;
else are they degenerate bastards, and apostates, reuolting from
the principals, and principall rules of sincere devotion. It is
not ynough for any man, that hath by long suit, tedious impre-
cations, jeopardous hazard, toyle of bodie, griefe of mind, piti-
full laments, obsequious fawnings, desperate passions, and passionate despaire, at length, for a meed or requitall to his unrest,
gained the favourable acceptance of his most, and best desired
ladie : it is not, I say, then, ynough for such a man to thinke,
that, by his pennance in obtayning, he hath performed a knight's
service having obtained ; but he must, thenceforth, as much
employ his industrie to preserue. For well sayd the poet,
whosoever sayd it—

Non minor est virtus quam quærere parta tueri.

Perfect service, and serviceable loyaltie, is seene more cleerely
in deseruing loue and maintaining it, than in attempting or
laboring for it. How can any one be sayd truely to serve,

when he more respects the libertie of his owne affections, than the imposition of ladies' command? To attaine happinesse, and then neglect it, is but an unhappie negligence, a negligent vnhappinesse: it is an vnthankfull ingratitude, than which nothing can be to heauen more hainous, and, in the regard of men, more detestable.

Herein are certain chuffes differing from the glorious nature of gentilitie, who, hauing stumbled vpon the raritie of beautie, are cloyed in their owne delicacies; not prizing the invaluable jewell of what they possesse, not esteeming the benefit of their precious felicitie, but, like swine towze pearle without respect, when as generous spirits glorie in their ample fortune, and subject themselues to their chiefest glorie; for, to be a de-seruing seruant to a deserued ladie, is liberally to enjoy heauen on earth. If, therefore, the scope of mortalitie consist in the fruition of imparadised content, or a contented paradise, how requisite is it, that knights (for under these titles of honour doe I conclude true louers) should loose the freedome of their owne wils, to be seruicable to the wils of their choycest ladies. Who can serve two masters? Who can be master of himselfe, when he is a seruant to his ladie, but either he scornes the humilitie due to her, or affects a singularitie to himselfe: if the one, he is no seruant; if the other, an vnfit louer. Why? for because a true louer must frame his actions to the behestes of his ladie, and magnifying her worthinesse. Hence is it sayd, and truely sayd, *knights in ladies seruice haue no free-will*: that is, they ought not to be theire owne, nor subject to their owne pleasure, vnlesse to please themselues in the recreation which tendeth to their ladies' honour. How pithily said a wise man—

Non amare decet, et amari præstat.

To loue is common to sensualitie, but to be beloued is the crowne of desert: they best deserue to be beloued who deserue loue; and they principally deserue loue who can moderate their private affection, and leuell the scope of desert to the executing

their ladies' commaund, and adorne their names by martiall
feates of armes : as for instance — Paris defended Hellen with
the losse of his life : Troylus would fight for Cresseida : Æneas
wonne Lavinia with the dint of his weapon and sweat of blood :
Pœlops hazarded his life for Hippodamia. Yea, what better
example than of late in our owne territorie ? that noble,
untimelie cropt spirit of honour our English Hector, who
cared not to undergoe any gust of spleene and censure, for his
neuer-sufficiently admired Opia, a perfect Penelope to her
ancient knight, Ulisses ; he an unfained Ulisses to her, for
whose sake neither the wiles of Circes, or inchauntments of
Syrens, or brunt of warrs, could force or intice to forgetfulnes.
But examples may seeme rather tedious than convenient : I
leaue the certainty of them to their authours, with this prouiso,
that what is manifest needs no commentarie. Now then, considering the perfections of ladies haue been, both in former and
moderne ages, so resonant through euery climate of the world,
what dull spirit, what leaden apprehension hath he, that
would be more curious, to vndertake the yoake of their seruice,
than forward to participate their beauties. Lentulus, the
Roman warrior, after all his conquests abroad, was willingly
captiv'd and conquered at home ; insomuch as, at the first
view of Terentia, hee fear'd not to say, *Non bellum, non fortuna :*
Fate cannot limitt, warre cannot subdue the efficacie of Loue.

> The fleeting pashions of disloyal minds
>   Proceeds from wrong directed scope of lust ;
> Inconstant chaunge beseems grosse-feeding hindes,
>   In whose deserts is neither faith or trust :
> When noble spirits in the bonds of dutie
> Pay tribute to the excellence of beautie.

> For gentle temper, of a freer blood,
>   Counts bondage to a ladie willing pleasure,
> Adoring seruice of best worthy good ;
>   And deeme their toile for favour pleasing leasure :

Not reckoning commaund seruilitie,
But true performance, true nobilitie.

To talke, conuerse, or dallie, is not loue,
    But amorous wantonesse of idle play :
Brunts of defence doth firme affection proue ;
    Who would not fight when beutie is the prey ?
Then, who is he who would not think hee's free,
When hee's inthral'd to loue's captivitie ?

Love's captiuitie is freedom's infranchisment, and whosoeuer
is a prisoner to the merrit of fairnesse is absolutely naturalized
a denizen to happines. To conclude (for in knowen verities
many proofes are needlesse), a true, and truely louing knight's
libertie, ought to be inchained to the disposure of his ladie : her
will must be to him a law, and that law not penall, but irre-
fragable. The sincerity of his tryed affection must bee an
obstacle to wilfulnes, with due consideration, that although he
be bound to vndergoe her pleasure, so he shall vndertake no
shame that may displease—for from the faire proceeds nothing
but what is faire. Ladies are mild, and fearefull to impose
dangers ; wise, and will preuent them : especially such daungers
as either may threaten inglorious dishonour, or likely perill
to their beloued. Timorous they are of the worst, carefull (and
in that care ambitious) for the best : Nature made them females,
vertuously kinde, women angellically vertuous : horror befits
not their sex, or vnthankfulnesse their beauties ; for although
warre defends the right of loue, yet loue cannot brooke the
severitie of warre,

    Dalliance in chambers, harmlesse play and sport,
    Doe with the sweetes of loue much better sort.

Since then, ladies are moulded of this temper, and tempered
in the mould of loue, mildnesse, and kindnesse, what is that
knight that would not be their captiue ? insomuch as the blunt-
est cynicke must in reason avow, that it is most reason that
knights in ladies seruice haue no free-will.

To the Right Honourable, the Earle of Arundel.

SECOND POSITION.

Beautie is the maintainer of Valour.

Right Honourable,

It is no predjudice to the precious charitie of knowledge, euen in undoubted truthes, to make truth more doubtles, for in matters of wrong arguments doe confound sence, when in explanation of right they doe senceably approoue it. 'Tis good ; mysterie in demonstration is a confused nicenesse : so knowne is the certainty of this position, *et domi, et foris*, that whosoeuer would seeme ignorantly strange, would but bewray his strangely rude ignorance in seeming so. Beautie (say we) is the maintayner of valour. Who is so blunt as knowes it not ? who is so blockish as will not (and may with justice) defend it ? an instance, euen in the entrance, shall bee no absurditie. In the infancie of the Romane Empire, (as Plutarch to the purpose rehearseth) the Romanes violently seazed vpon the Sabines ladies : by violence they wonne them, by valour they justified their winning ; insomuch as euer after, betwixt these warlike nations, began both increase of hatred, and defiance of hostilities. In which times kissing had his first originall, devised by the Sabine ladies as an earnest-peny of desart to the guerdon of the Romanes desperate toyle. For although, in the eyes of some more stoicall censures, kissing seems but a needlesse ceremonie, yet, in the feeling of loue, it is the first tast of loue, the first certaintie of hope, the first hope of obtaining, the first obtaining of favour, the first favour of graunt, the first graunt of assurance, the first and principallest assurance of affection, the first shadow of the substance of after contented happinesse, happy pleasure, pleasing heauen. But to our matter : men for the most part (some more heroycall inclinations by nature excepted) are, in the frailtie of their humanitie, so fearefull of harmes, and so desirous of the preseruatiue of life, as although not the discouragement of cowardise, yet proper instinct of mortalitie, will deter them from wilfull and imminent running into perill. Some, againe, are of that frozen and cold temperature of disposition as, according to the prouerbe, they esteeme it prouident safetie to sleepe in a whole skinne. Of this imbecilitie are many, who have only enioyed the lazie softnesse of vitious ease, and neuer felt, at least neuer conceited, the touch of any miserie, no nor of gentilitie. The selfe alone meanes, therefore, that were to be ordayned for a prouocation and incitement to liuelihood of manhood was the quintessence, raritie, yea, rare quintessence of divine astonishment, Beautie : upon whose al-perfection the greedy eye of desire (euen in spirits of clay and mud) being fixt, hath stir'd up such a rauishment of possession, as they now esteeme all dangers weake ; nay, all impossibilities facilities to possesse it. That cardinall-vertue of inuincible fortitude had long since ben level'd with cowardise, had not beauty, the alarum to magnanimitie, rent the distrust of weaknes, and strengthened it with contempt of precedencie, æmulation of desert. Say, then, how probable is it, how indubitate hereditary is the dependance of valor to the merit of beauty ? Beautie ! which prickes on the slowest, encourageth the faint-harted, sharpens the dull, commaundeth the stowtest, recreateth the wearie, and guerdoneth the deseruing. Beautie ! the largesse of the gods ; the comfort of men ; the bounty of heauen ; the prize of earth ; the paradise of glory ; the *via lactea* to felicitie ; the wonder of itselfe—Beautie. This is that Achilles impenetrable shield, which euerie Ulisses pleads for, euery Ajax fights for ; this is that golden fleece, which the Argonants sued to find, which Iason toyling enioied. This is that famoused trophey, which Philip would haue his sonne

Alexander in the games of Olympus to wrastle for. How much are they deceived (I mean those fainter bloods) who vainly imagine that souldiers fight for spoile only ; generals hazard their persons for greedines ; sea men trafique for auarice ; knights wander for prey, or that any ieopards his life chiefly for lucre. Does not the marchant venture ship-wrack to returne with a present that may purchase his ladie's liking, and in her liking his owne blisse ? Does not the souldier fight abroad to preserue his ladie in safety at home ? Does not the generall commaund that he may returne with victorie gracious in his ladie's eyes ? Does not the knight-errant attempt threatnings of horrour, aduentures of dread, thunder of death it selfe, onely to rumour his fame in the eares of his ladie ? Does he not range for the succour of beautie ? for the freedome of beautie ? for the ioy of beautie ? and all spoyle that the souldier bleedes for, all the greedinesse that commaunders sweat for, all the auarice that the marchant trades for, all the prey that the knight aduentures for, all the benefite that euerie one and all these hope, wish, pray, contend for, is the fruition of Beautie ; than which nothing can be more gratefull, nothing is so acceptable.

Valour. Through streames of blood, and massacres of death,
I spend the troubles of a glorious breath :
In feates of armes and life's dread desperation,
I touze to gaine me fame and reputation.
All that I strive for is to comprehend
Honour ; to honour all my labours tend.

Honour. Valour doth aime at me, I aime at Beautie,
And make my greatnes greater by my dutie :
Valour doth fight for me, when all my prize
Consists in favour of sweet Beauties eies.
Honour sustaineth valour : when againe
Beautie feedes honour, and in that them twaine.

Beautie. Mean-bred deserts who covet much ambition,
   Hauing attain'd it, euer grow ambitious,
Soring to gaine my loue, in whose tuition
   Their greatnes is aduanst, and made propitious.
I strengthen cowards, and exalt the spirits
   Of weaknesse ; I maintaine proud chiualrie,
In me the drifts of honour pledge their merits,
   To guerdon and discerne worthes dignitie ;
And but for me they brunts of hazard loath :
Honour payes Valour ; Beautie rules them both.

The whole scope that Valour and men of valiant courage ayme their drifts at is, for the most part, a famous name and reputed honour ; but the marke which honour directs his level to is to participate the delightfull sweets of sweetest beautie ; which in all succeeding posterities hath been of so powerfull and powerfully respected awe, that for the hopes which men haue euermore conceived of enjoying it, they haue with accoutrements of defence been prest, for feare of losing, to preserve it. Beautie ! why it is the life of magnanimitie, it is the perfect sparke, whose lustre reflecteth boldnesse to the timorous. Beautie ! what is it ? what can it else be, but the modell of all fortitude ? for this proofe (unlesse I be mistaken, as I am not) did the antiquaries of the elder world, such as were Martialists, attribute all worship vnto Pallas, all adoration to Bellona, reverencing her as the goddesse of armes, yet shee a woman. Fayre she was, els in vaine would shee strive with Venus for the golden ball : valiant she was, els with foolish superstition did the ancient best warriors adore her, and the younger Sophyes allow her. Yes, yes ; she was wise, beautiful, and valiant, including this morrall, that as shee had courage, so was shee a woman, whose force was not more fierce to terrifie, but her beautie was as piercing to wound. Did they applaud her martiall disposition ? True ; but they did reverence her amiable looks : most certain it is, the valiant may

and do contend with the valiant, but Beautie hath the maistery
of both.

Audentes forma cogit audaces.

Loue breaths more resolution into the forwardnes of the resolued ; for neuer have we read, neuer heard of any undaunted
champion, who, being free in his owne affections, did strive so
much by perillous exployts to adorne the rumour of fame, but,
if he after were blest by being an entertained seruant to some
worthy ladie, those daungers, which before seemed dangers, he
would now deem easie, and all easy atchievements toyes, onely
that should then bee most honorable, which threatned most
terror.   Hercules valued the swimming ouer the sea, to breed
wonder in Deianeira, not for that he desired to doe it, but because she should admire and commend the deed.   Why do
spruce courtiers practize courtlike actiuitie ? but to breed delight to their ladies.   Why doe men in generall contend to
excel in brauerie ? but to be noted the brauest of their ladies.
Why doe cormorants hoord treasure ? but to attract some
ladies liking.   Why do poore men toyle ? great men trauerse ?
but all to one end — to share Beautie.   Why doe kings and
greatest princes thirst to enlarge their empires and dominions ?
but to be noted for more eminent, and more to be loued for
that eminence of their ladies.   Let vs looke into all the de-
voyres of mankind, and they all tend to the content of beautie.
Men to honour men, is rather a bootlesse feare, then in
regardfull loue ; but for men to bee honoured of ladies, is
the scope of all felicitie.   Men in kindnesse are mutually lambs,
but in corriual-shipp of loue lyons.   Should I fight for my
friend, I might be appeazed in my choller ; but for my lady, I
am inexorable.

Chalibs mihi circa pectus.

The teares of widows, the cries of babes, the condolement of
parents, the intreaties of children, the wounds of the maimed,
the wracke of the oppressed, cannot moue pity in a steeled

hart, which fights for report in the honor of his lady. It is said of the Turks, they traine their youth in discipline of warre, with intent of cruelty ; beleeue it, I cannot be perswaded that, beeing so absolute warriors, they shuld so wholy be mur-therous tyrants, except to returne with triumph in the sight of their ladies. Tamburlaine, the scourge of God, and sauadgest monster of his time, neuer made a slaughter upon any of his conquered captives, but the principallest he euer sent as slaues to his queene Zenocrate, intending that, as she was the deity who infused strength into his armes, so shee should be the whole glory of his tryumph.

> *Pax ruat in bellam, sociumqs in prælia fœdus :*
> *Causa subits nulla fronte regendus amor.*

How requisite it is, then, for a kingdom which would be for-tifyed with choyce of magnanimous spirits, to be also inriched with the ornament of beauty, the expediency in occasions of necessity makes evident. I haue often marvailed why the Romanes (famous for their loues) going to battaile against a world of so many nations as they did, for more suerty of vic-tory had not carried their ladies with them, that by the sight of them their enfeebled strength might (like the head of Hydra) doubly haue renued. Doubtles, had Julius Cæsar, at his first arrival for the conquest of Britaine, brought with him Cleo-patra, he would neuer haue twise suffered so shamefull a re-pulse. What infinite examples might here be alledged for the probation, that beauty hath euermore instigated audacity to the dullest ! finally, in the apprehension of common reason, let euery man examine himselfe, whether it be not the immediate norisher of al fortitude. It is, it hath been, and euer will be the nurse and foode of heroicall chiualry ; for valour, not seasoned with the hopes of loue, is an irresolute valour.

A souldier, and libertine, is an unarmed souldier. Beauty is the spur to honor, honor the serviceable attendant on beauty : yet will some home-bred poring academicke say, it is the only

means to make a warrior a flat coward ; for beauty allures to
delights, delights to ease, ease consequently the fosterer to dis-
couraged pusillanimity : but let such an inexperienced plodder
knowe, it is as difficult for him to censure of courage, as it is
easy for the couragious to scorne his censure, or indeed rather
pittie his ridiculous folly in censuring ; as Hannibal did Phormio,
when he would read him a lecture of war, who had euer bin
trained in the wars : as if a mild louer may not dally at home
in a cabinet, yet the selfe same be a severe souldier in the field.
Let, therefore, euery man of reason be reasonable in vnderstanding, and, where he cannot contradict, confesse that the
truth is greatest, and chiefly prevaileth, principally when armes
will justifie what arguments confirme, and arguments againe
reciprocally corroborate what armes (on the behalfe of justice)
doth mantaine, and rightly mantaine, that merely of it selfe
Beauty is the maintainer of Valour.

To the Right Honorable the Earle of Pembroke.

THIRD POSITION.
Faire Ladie was neuer false.

RIGHT HONORABLE.

The temperature of the mind follows the temperature of the bodie—which certaine aciome (sayes that sage prince of philosophers, Aristotle) is euer more infallible. Then, doe not I a little marvell what arrogant spleen of malediction, with teeth of juyceles envie, durst to detract from the worthines of beauty; terming it a particular blessing, bestowed for a more general curse; terming it fickle, deceitfull, inconstant, when, if the sawes of authority be authentical, nothing can be more precious, nothing in it selfe more vertuous. Faire Ladie was neuer false. Oh! sayes some curious impostor, *Euge hominem!* a goodly theame: much witt no doubt expected: few proofes produced. who will not sweare the contrary? who will not beleeue the contrarie as his creed? Vaine fondlings, as many as so beleeue, doubtlesse shall be so deceiued, and doe penance for their errour in the gall of their distrust. For, if the temperature of the mind follow the temperature of the bodie, (text it is) then, without controuersie, as the outward shape is more singular, so the inward vertues must be more exquisite. Nature is but the handmayd to heauen: beautie is the rarest workemanship of Nature's power. So, questionlesse, where the hand-maid of heauen hath imparted her art, the blessings of the gods are plentifully abounding. Neither will they make that lame which Nature hath framed perfect. For why? Can falsehood lye hidden under the raritie of fairnesse? No more than vice can lurke under the plumes of vertue, which is meerely impossible. Beautie is but a faire inne to lodge more

fairer guests within : it is but the liuely colour of an excellent
tasting wine : it is the greatest good in it selfe that heart of
humanitie can wish for.   If deformitie be the dregs and scum
of earth's disgrace ; if it be (as it is) the curse of the parents
transgression layd upon the child ; then, contrarily, must
beautie be the immediate testimonie of heauen's fauor ?   Why
were people, in times past, called giants and monsters, but for
the ugly appearance of their shapes ?   neither were they in
body so mishapen, as in conditions odious.   So, then, euen in
them it is manifestly verified, that foulest enormities harbour
in fowlest formes ; then, it followes, that firmest vertues are
shrowded in the fairest complexions.   Some, indeed, oppose an
argument that beauty of it selfe is a great good, but the abuse
most wretched and common — yea, so common, that the very
face of beautie is a presumption ; yea, more, a warrant of in-
constancie.   To such is easily replyed—Such abuse proceeds
not from perfect beautie, but from the adulterate counterfeit of
beautie, art.   Of this nature are those that, being intemperately
wanton, strive, with artificiall cunning, to cover the defects of
nature ; for true beautie, as it is of itselfe a good, so is it in
it selfe simple, innocent, and harmlesse, into which no thought
of vnkindnesse can penetrate ; and, being once subiect to loue,
can neuer, will neuer be tempted to loosnesse.   O strange !
sayes one ! oh, heresie ! cries another ; palpably false, falsely
absurd !   Do not poets, the pillars of your folly, affirme that
Venus, forsooth your only deity of your passions, the queen of
your thoughtts, the boast and goddesse of your loues, was absolutely false to her husband ? else had Cupid been vnborne ;
Æneas vnbegotten.   And yet, lady was neuer fair and false !
Was not Helen of Greece made a Trojan stale — a scorne to
posterities—whose verie name is ominous to cuckolds ? Do not
all chronicles of antiquity shew, not only that the faire, but the
fairest, haue prooued lightest ? and yet, faire ladie was neuer
false !   True ; the poets say so, who, being themselves lascivi-
ously addicted, thought it great inhumanity, at least injurie,

that beautie shuld be ingrost to the proper vse of one alone
man. Besides, if poets are to be credited, Venus was a goddesse, not framed by nature, but yssuing from the gods, and
therfore aboue human apprehension.   Poets speak truth to
warrant their writs, and so was Venus faire : they deuise fictions
to approue their wits, so was she immodest : with this caveat,
that she was Venus was a troth, that she was trothles a
fiction.   Also Helen was counted faire, because many affected
her, procur'd by her enticing wantones, inviting allurements.
Curteous I thinke she was, and therfore beloued ; faire neuer,
for then not fickle. Indeed, I acknowledge, old writers being
themselues past the youth of loue, and sunk into dotage, haue
inveighed against the dignity of that sex, not vpon knowledg,
but mere supposition, deming that because the worst are haunted
of the worst for their lewdnes, condemne the fairest for being
faire, as the principall inchantment.   Now, so much difference
is there betwixt the wanton and the faire, as the wanton may
be beloued, but the faire wil not be wanton.   It is to be supposed, that such as inclined to the loose ficklenesse of change
are not of that excellent temper of true bewty, because then
they, knowing their own merit, (as women of that nature do)
wold be by how much the more noted, by so much the more
tender of the preseruation of the honors report, and somewhat precizely (pardon troth) prize their own value : *Scire
tuum nihil est, nisi te scire hoc sciat alter.*   To be faire and not
admired is as a hidden minerall, yet, to be admired, and not
preserue that admiration, is an unvalued indignity. But, as
ladies are fair, so are they wise ; and as they are both faire and
wise, constant. Alas ! most know, and many fele, that bewty
is not easily woed to loue ; many bitter conflicts of oppressed
griefs are to be indured, ere they are won to listen to affection.
And, at length being persuaded, they were not so obdurat before to be sued to, as they are now most constant in their loues,
most sincerely firme to their choice. Experience teacheth it,
that stele is not soon hot ; yet, being once fired, is lesse easily

cooled. An example or two shal warrant the credit of the rest.
Who could bee more industrious to his ladie, than Theseus was
in gaining Ariadne? Who, being conquered, was euer most
fast to him, though injuriously, yea, perfidiously forsaken of
him? Portia so inderely reuerenced Cato, as she would for his
preseruation swallow coles. — Alcest wold die for Admetus;
and Penelope (the mirror of the Greeke matrons, both for
constancy and bewty) wold neuer falsify her faith to Ulisses.
I my self shuld account such proofs inconuenient, did not the
proofe of my defence rely vpon former instances, compared both
with present and latter times. Diana, renowned for beauty,
was more renowned for chastity, insomuch as singularly and
truly fairest ladies contended to be her nymphs, if trust to
writers may be attributed : *rara præclara ;* according to the
proverbe, that the fairest are the fairest, that is, the best and
best to be estemed. What is more to be vrged for the rati-
fying our maintenence, but the exterior beauty is assurance of
the interior quality. To answere to euery vain objection, that
some more nice wits, only seeming witty in censure and miscon-
struction, is not here intended, as *fronti nulla fides :* the ficklenes
of Cresseida ; the mutability of some Lais : let it suffice,
they are fictions and nugatory invectiues of deseruingly abused
poets, or repulsed annalogers, ridiculous in the understanding
of the wise, contemptible in the perseuerance of understanding.
It is euen as impossible for ladies of quaintest formes to incline
to thoughts of trothles impudency, as for monsters of deformity
to produce effects of vertue. Needs there any other demonstration then the admirable (almost incredible) ornament of
chastity, Lucrece, the Roman dame, the paragon of those
times, the mirror of those daies, for rauishing perfection of
beauty? harmles, unspotted Lucrece, who did withstand lust
to the eternizing of her honor, and monumented her rape with
extremity of death! Who is he so obstinate in his errour,
so wilful in his madnes, so mad in his erronious wilfulnes,
as would not euen in the glas of Lucresia's perseuerance (euen

to the vttermost extinct of life) se the wonder of bewty matched
with the indiuiduat adjunct, unsoyled constancy.

Constantia est gemella venustatis individua.

Three particularities there are that stand firme for this position ; examples already alledged, approbation of judgement
newly rehearsed, and ground of troth now to be verefi'de—
Verefi'de, said I ? the self assurance of the subject is a testimony most probable : if vice be the nourisher of vice, vertue
must be the effect of vertue. That is sincerely a vertue, which
is a good, and that good is beauty ; so herein fictions comprehend truth, as *forma bonum.* Yet ere I wade further, and
be grauel'd in the owze, and quicksand of my own intention,
I am for clearing of such as may misconceite my drift, to
make an apology for my defence : neither by my iust iustifica-
tion of an apparant verity, the wanton shall taxe my indevours
as ridiculous, knowing their own imperfections, nor challenge
this as a due belonging to the encouragement of their lenity.
I confesse (and blush that occasion should be ministred of confession) that many there are whose bewitching lookes drawe
youth into folly, and age into dotage, rather madnes : too
many there are whose smooth counterfeit, in the indiscretion of
virility, may passe for beauty, when the counterfeiters are so
mutable, as they are neither euer their own, or euer certaine any
on's. Yea, euen in great personages this loosenesse is an im-
boldening to the meaner, rather a president to the worst of
offending ; the greatnes of their estates, (I speake of some that
haue beene) bolstereth out the community of licentious immo-
desty, whose shames, were they enameled in the tableture of
their foreheads, it would be a hideous visour to more deformed
complections, more enormious conditions. Such these are,
who, vnder the abhomination of luxury, (nicely termed kindnes)
import the pretexted glosse of beauties name, to such are also
mercenarye slaues, intimated servants, against whom, although
my purpose is not inueigh, yet doe I here exclude them from

out the assotiation of the faire : let those be false ; beautifull they are not. In them the temperature of the body follows the temperature of the mind, not the temperature of the mind, the temperature of the body ; of whom the philosopher insisteth. As I said before, so I here avow, that the error of their enchanting amyablenes bewitcheth their adherents, who, being ensnared in the nets of their lasciuousnes, esteeme that prime beauty which they themselues deliciously enjoy. For, as the loose haue no substance but fading art to attract, so the excellently faire haue no falsehood to be soyled, no cunning to beguile, no visor to delude. They are doues without gals ; swans without spots ; fawnes without spleene : they are simple, and will not be trained ; faire and cannot be tempted : they are the pure color of white, without staine, whose delicate eares, by prophaned tongues, may bee enforced to heare ill, but whose unmoued breasts by the fond cannot be enflamed to consent to il. Herein are the bewtiful, said to be angels on earth, for that, as they exceed others in wonder of beauty, so they excell all other in graces of vertue : it shall not be amisse to answere to the maleuolent will of some witty maleuolent detractors :

Adverse.

Women ! O they are fickle falling starres ;
  Tydes in their ebbes, moones euer in the wayne,
Frost in the thawe, faint hearted in the wars
  Of constancy, yet constant in disdaine.
Women ! O they are creatures most unholly,
Borne for a scourge to men, and curbe to folly.
          Mulieri ne credas, ne mortuæ quidem.

Proofe.

Women ! why they are fixed lamps of heauen,
  Shining bright lustre to the hearts of men,
Firme diamonds, and faire, bright lookes, hearts euen,
  Constant in scorne of motions, where and when.

Princes for ladies praise haue fell at odds ;
They are of men ador'd, belou'd of gods :
The highest blessing that to earth's vncommon
Is man's perfection, soule of life, a woman.

Diis compares fœminœ.

Euery faire lady is louely, but euery louely ladye is not faire :
so then the lovely may be fickle, but the faire cannot be inconstant. What should I more say ; and yet what haue I saide
that is inough ? What that can bee too much, and yet what is
not to much ? since the only experience of the subject com-
mendeth his own worthines. To such, then, as credit it,
I wish them a faire lady : to misbelevers and infidels in loue
this curse :—may their ladies be foule, and so be loathsome, yet
false, and repay them with the common crest of hornes.

To the Right Honourable the Earle of Mountgomery.

THE FOURTH AND LAST POSITION.

Perfect louers are onely wise.

RIGHT HONOURABLE.

Perspicax est amatorum vigilans ocellus, prævidet adversa, studet horis convenientibus. A perfect louer is neuer lesse idle, then when he is idle ; neuer more busied, then when least seriously imployed.

Wise seeming censors count that labour vaine
 Which is deuoted to the hopes of loue,
 When they themselues themselves much vainer proue,
By holding lovers labours in disdaine :
They haue forgot the wiles which made them tremble
 In heat of youth, when youth their bloods did moue,
What wit they vsed, what teares they did dissemble.

Their now waxt shallow apprehensions, then
 Were quick to see the worst, wise to preuent it :
 How they pleas'd fancie, how they might content it,
How much their hearts differed from hearts of men :
How prouident they were to fawne, to flatter,
 To sweare, vow, vrge their griefe, and to lament it :
Alas ! who would not doo't in such a matter ?

Loue makes men wise : 'tis not a feeling kisse
That's the true sport ; ther's sport more sweet than this,
To which, ere louers throughly doe attaine,
They must attend, doe service, grieve, and faine.
For this with ladies' honours best doth fit,
Not to be conquered by desire, but witt.

In all ages, both past and present, neuer haue there beene more witty pollicies, more politicke circumventions broached then in speedie obtaining of delatorie loue; which is in itselfe so vrgent, so impatient of delayes, as the soundest sleights, quaintest deuises, haue beene studied for accomplishing of rest to vnrest, ease to disquiet, remedy to desperation. Three things triall hath taught to be expedient for mastery in love:—after choice, patience is to indure reproofes, witt to procure content, boldnesse to attempt at opportunities. Vaine is patience without hope; hope desperate without meanes; meanes, when occasion proffers, her forelock, and women toleration, hinderance without boldnesse. Yet boldnesse without witte is to no vse; neither without witte shall time be euer found when to be bold. In a perfect lover, therefore, all these three are judicially cohered. Also, if a curious surveior will upon this approve that louers have beene witty, yet disallow any wisedom in this witt, by distinguishing a different discrepancie betwixt witt and wisdome, since the one tendeth onely to folly of humanity, the other to consideration of diuinity, I will answer, that perfect lovers, even in this respect, are perfectly wise; as with ease thus. Being ouercome with the affection of some excellently deseruing beauty, with admiration of the singular perfection thereof, with what curious workmanship it is framed, with what glorye of majesty it is endowed, it is an immediate occasion, to bring them in serious conceit of weighing the wonders of the heauens in compacting such admirable quintessence in so precious a forme, by which they will deepely revolue the dignitye of God in that mould, and truely acknowledge the weaknesse of their owne nature in comparison of beauty. This is the ready and directest course to force men to consider their owne frailty, and magnifie the omnipotency of their Creator in fashioning both: so as love is the onely line which leadeth man to the font of wisedome; that is, to the gloryfying of heauen's power, and confessing man's imbecillity. Who then can deny, who will not allowe, that perfect louers are onely wise? onely wise? true;

or men devoted to contemplation of theologie, are withdrawne
from the absolute and due reuerence (sometime, of him to whome
they chiefly owe all due reuerence by humane affaires ; when
louers haue euermore the idea of beauty in their imaginations,
and therefore hourely do adore their Maker's architecture.   Perfect louers are onely wise.   Now againe to humanity : the dullest
wit, the most vnseasoned capacity, being once salted with the
tast of loue, sharpens his dulnesse, and seasons his capacity, to
study any sleight, any deuice for setting a period to his desires :
insomuch, as no time shall euer present any opportunity of
study, but all inuention is vsed, all conceiptes imployed, for the
fruition of his beloued ; who beeing injoyed, yet his wittes are
neuer idle, but industrious for conseruation of what hee inioyes,
as loath to impart from that which with so much vigilancie he
not easily obtained.   As hitherto I haue proceeded with demonstration of examples, so now (to the purpose) will I inferre an
instance to the more effectual proofe of this.   The Greekes,
after the discursion of Helen, preparing an expedition against
Troy, both for acquittance of their injury, and recouery of their
false (neuer truly faire) queene, stood not in more need of
Achilles for his courage, then of Ulisses for his counsaile ; who
being then newly married to his perfectly faire Penelope, was
vpon good cause moued (in the tendernesse of his loue) unwil-
ling to that action.   But excuse could not preuaile, except pollicie
could find excuse : he feares much, but loues more ; which loue,
euen at an instant, ripens his invention : loue ripeneth his invention ; he faines madnesse, and for madnesse to aduise in sober
actions would proue but a mad aduice, an vnaduised madnesse :
but he was discouered and went.   Secondly, what vndoubted
wisdom in him did charme his eares against the incantations of
the Syrens ; the devoute affection which he bore to his Penelope quickning his apprehension.   Was euer man a truer louer,
and euer man more truly wise ?   It is infallibly certaine, certainly infallible, perfect louers are onely wise.   Now it may be
cauelled that that cannot be, for how can louers be wise, when

loue it selfe is both vaine, idle, and foolish ; a toye, a meere conceit of fancie ? But how vaine, foolish, idle, and fantastical, are they that so conceiue ! Loue is the onely band, the alone obligation, that traffiques betwixt earthly creatures and heauenly angels, that vnites woman to man, yea man to man, nay man to himselfe, and himselfe to God. Loue is the dignity of man's worth, not a blind Cupid, a sensual lust, as poets faine ; but an earnest and reasonable desire of good, as authorities confirme. It is an entire conjunction of soules together.

> *Mutua sors animi, pia commutatio mentis,*
> *Sub fido fidum est pectore pignus amor.*
> *Quid magis est placidum ? nihil est fœlicius illo ;*
> *Pax jucunda, manus splendida, tuta quies.*
> *Fulget in auricoma nitido cum robore forma :*
> *Ipsa sua splendens gaudet amore Venus.*

> Loue is that tickling blood, which softly creepes
>   Into the pleasures of a quiet brest ;
> Presenting pretty dreames in slumbring sleepes,
>   And in a ladie's bosome takes his rest.
> Loue baths him in the channel of delight,
> Which louers sigh for, and wish they also might.

> Of twenty thousand 'tis the wittiest passion,
>   Wise in foreseeing of ensuing care ;
> Makes louers prouident, yeelds consolation,
>   And checks the bad from ill, if so they dare.
> Loue is that fountaine, where the springs do lye,
> Whence sweetest waters run, yet neuer drie.

> Loue is that harmlesse prick in pleasant brier,
> Which doth most please the sent, and breed desire.

Thus much for the satisfaction of the witty. Now, briefly followes a conclusion to the wise. Louers are perfectly wise,

and simply perfect ; indeed, absolutely perfect, insomuch as nothing is more expedient to the full accomplishment of a wise
man, then to be a louer.   Now, would any man seeme to oppose himselfe to the adverse maintaining of what hath already
been prooved, it will be euident he shall more toyle his braines
to affirme an vntroth, then the praise or commendation hee ex-
pects with a generall plaudite will counteruaile.   If any champion will likewise be desperate hardy to vndertake a disallowance
of these challenged positions, question lesse he neede not doubt
but he shall not soner be armed, but as soone foyled, and in
the vulgar confession of shame acknowledge his deerely bought
wilfulnesse.   But I leaue that to triall : I heere meane to be a
pen man, no champion.

CONCLUSION.

Would any man be gracious in a ladie's favour ? let him,
then, subject himselfe to her wil.   Would any be valiant and
renowned for chiualry ? let him serue vnder the colours of
beauty.   Would any striue to be blessed in hauing a lady truly
constant ? let him choose her truly faire.   Would any be perfectly wise ? let him be perfectly louing.   Would any be
happy, couragious, singular, or prouident ? let him be a louer.
In that life consisteth all happinesse, all courage, all glory, all
wisdome.   But as for such who doe *frigescere ad ignem*, I do desist
to inveigh against their cold spirits ; onely in this I hate them,
that I pitty them.

> He who will striue to please each curious eye
> Must freeze in silence ; but I care not I :
> Let better favours favour mine indeuour,
> The vulgar tauntings shall affright me neuer.
> May it please you, to whom it is intended,
> Then,
> 'Tis glory to deserve, though not commended.

Non omnibus studeo : non malevolis.

FINIS.

THE

MONARCHS MEETING,

OR

The King of Denmarkes welcome into England.

Now had the harvest of the yeare brought forth
 The blessed frute of long expected hope,
And leveld with the toile of labours worth
 The crop of fatnesse to the trad's-man scope:

Now were the blossomes ripened to the hand
 Of well deserving sweat; when all anon
The mighty ruler of a peaceful land
 Began to take his wisht progression.

Calme was the sea, and gentle gustes did blow
 A whistling gale unto the flagges of peace:
Full were the streames, and smooth soft tides did flow,
 And gave assurance of contented ease;

When on bubbling beauty of fayre Thames
 (Urg'd by the princely loue of amitie)
 A Christian king in state and majestie
Was entertain'd with sundry showes of games.

The siluer crystal streame was proud to beare
 The burthen of a person, each way graced
With all the rites of humane loue and feare,
 In whose high lookes honour was lively placed.

D

Much welcome was the tydings of this newes
   Unto the royall eare of worthy James,
Preparing with all speed, that speed might vse,
   With his owne presence to ennoble Thames.

Looke how did Ioue salute the minor gods,
   Inuiting all in heauen at a feast,
Where no more was reuerenc'd, no odds
   Betwixt his proper person and the rest :

So did these princes meet, in whose first meeting
   Joy was aboundant in the truce of love ;
Each inter-changing a concordant greeting,
   Which in the peeres of both did comfort move.

Ambitious was the riuer of this honour,
   Knowing the value of the weight she bore :
Grac'd that such favour kings bestow'd upon her,
   Bearing a richer burthen nere before.

Kings met, and kings saluted one another,
   Eyther rejoycing in the others sight ;
Princes with princes, brother ioy'd with brother,
   Each solacing the other with delight.

A goodly view of majestie it was
   To see such intimated league betwixt them :
They striv'd in kindnesse how they might surpasse,
   Sporting the season which the tide prefixt them.

Like to a prince, in euery point aright,
   He came, and like a prince was entertained
With all the tipes of dignity bedight,
   With all the friendship friendship could haue claimed.

O, what a gladsome sight of joye it is,
    When monarches so are linkt in amitie !
How strengthened are those empires with safe blisse,
    Where two such princes joyne in unitie !

Great both are in dominions, yet more great
    In being vertuously religious :
Fresh blooming piety doth praise beget
    In goodly zeale.   Let tyrants be litigious.

What he amongst the stoutest of contempt,
    Full in command, and fuller in disdaine,
Durst any threats of enmity attempt,
    Or to oppose himselfe against those twaine ?

Those twaine ! so firmly are they matcht together,
    So euerlastingly affectionate,
So indiuidually combin'd together,
    As they loue none of both, who do one hate.

Power with power, realme with realme united,
    Hearts joyn'd with hearts, and hand imbrac'd in hand :
Should all the world of nations be excited,
    Yet all the world could scarce those two withstand.

Nor is it faining shew of smooth pretext,
    But doubtlesse troth of loue which brought him hither :
Let none with such suspition be perplext,
    For then they neuer had thus come together.

Nor can it be suppos'd a prince so mighty,
    So worthy in himselfe, so absolute,
Who hath so large a rule, a charge so weighty,
    Would leave his countrie but for meere repute.

Puissant is the Danish king, and strong
    In all the sinews of approved force :
Valiant and able for to right the wrong,
    That should proceed from any eager course.

It is no common thing, seene euery day,
    Scarce in an age, to see so great a state,
From out his countries boundes to come away,
    For visitation of an neighbouring mate.

It is no common honour that is done
    Unto our happy land by his arriving :
Much worth thereby and glory haue we won,
    Our home-bred hearts, with stranger loves reuiving.

Two kings in England have beene rarely seene,
    Two kings for singularitie renowned ;
The like before hath hardly euer beene,
    For never were two with more honour crowned.

This may we boast, and after times report
    How much the king of Denmarke grac'd our age ;
A king of so much eminence, such port,
    By his arrival did his love ingage.

England with Denmarke, Denmarke eke with us,
    Are firmly now in league, conioyned in one :
Seven kingdomes now againe united thus
    Are strength'ned, so as stronger can be none ;
Then, as a certaine and welwishing greeting,
We thus applaud the monarch's happy meeting.

Hayle, princely stemme of great magnificence !
Issue of royall blood, who dost commence
True instance of thy fast undoubted loue,
And by thy comming certainely approue
The pledge of peace, thus low in humblest heart,
Regreetes vnto thy truce doe we impart.
With fit applause, our thankes deuoutly running
Gives welcome to the honour of thy comming :
Time cannot rase, nor amity surcease
Betwixt our realme and thine a long liv'd peace :
Whiles thoughts are undefil'd and credit true,
From age to age this league will still renue ;
And thou thyselfe (great King of Danes) wilt joy,
Counting the hazards which thou didst imploy,
Daungers of thankes, by tasting approbation
Of spotlesse friendship with our willing nation.
We are not subtile French, to fawne and flatter ;
Nor Spaniards, hot in shew, yet cold in matter :
Trothlesse Italian, fleeting Irish wiles,
(Whose trust when most protesting most beguiles)
We deeme dishonour Germaine policies ;
Or everchanging Indian fopperies,
We spurne.　Know we are English, hating wrongs,
Bearing our thoughts decipher'd in our tongs :
Rather the sunne may in his courses alter,
Then we in true-meant trust our promise faulter.
Which of our chiefest emulating foes
Can justly taxe us ?　But we euer chose
To die with fame then live with infamy,
Purchas'd with disesteemed trechery :

What needs an instance? rumor will avow
We haue our troth ingrauen in our brow—
" Who are in nature false, yet free in name,
" Are servile slaves to feare, and fooles to shame."
What more? we are thy friends, and thou art our,
Thy loue is ours, and our force thy power:
Long may this happy thred of faith be woven,
And nere have dissolution but with heaven.
Fatall and joyous doth the knot begin,
Then, who doth breake it first commits first sin.
Lo! then, great monarch, with what words of zeale
Thy comming wee imbrace, and hopes reveale
Of linkt conjunction, prest to gratifie
That loue, which thou with loue dost ratifie.
Here speakes the clamour of a public voyce,
Which speaking, all doe publikly rejoyce
Thy safe arrivall.   England thankes the honour,
Which by thy presence thou bestowest vpon her,
Sounding lowd ecchoes of thy kingly fame,
And making trophees to adorne thy name.
The clarion's breath thy welcome, bells do ring,
Praise shoutes, whiles all thy friends thus sweetly sing.

THE APPLAUSE SONG

FOR THE

KING OF DENMARKES ARRIVAL.

In the most happy season of the yeare,
   When fayrest sun-shine glistered on the earth,
The royall king of Denmarke did appeare,
   And tun'd the hearts of England full with mirth :
In goodly maiesty, and princely cheere,
Euen in the fullest crop of harvests birth,
When birdes with pleasant notes did sweetly sing,
To giue a hearty welcome to the king.
     Prettily, prettily,
      With musick sweet,
     Did Philomele merily
      And ioyfully,
     And euer prettily
  The noble king of Denmarke greet.
Welcome to England, prince of high degree,
And all our song shall euer welcome be.

Our king himselfe rejoyced in his sight ;
His presence to the Court did breed delight ;
Blithe was the country and the citty proud—
Cornets with trumpets shrill did blow, and lowd,
     To welcome to our land
      With hearty greeting,
    (By our king's command)
     The monarches meeting :

Which we fulfilling
With loue and mindes willing,
Ioyn'd together :
Welcome hither,
    Friendly,
    And ever
    Kindly,
The Danish king, a prince of high degree,
For all our song shall ever welcome bee :
To welcome all our notes, and loue doth tend,
In that sence we began, with that we end.

Cantibus, et carmine.

FINIS.

A

LINE OF LIFE.

Pointing out the Immortalitie

of a

Vertuous Name.

Printed by W. S. for N. Butter, and are
to be sold at his shop neere
Saint Austens gate.

1620.

WISE, AND THEREIN NOBLE.

Ambition, beeing sooner discovered by acting then plotting, can rarely personate practise in studie, unlesse the arts themselues, which in themselues are liberall, should be too curiously censured, too inquisitiuely confined. It is an easie vanity, in these dayes of libertie, to be a conceited interpreter, but a difficult commendation to bee a serious author; for, whatsoeuer is at all times honestly intended, oftentimes is too largely construed. Generall collections meet (not seldome) with particular applications, and those so dangerous, that it is more safe, more wise, to professe a free silence then a necessarie industrie.

Here in this (scarce an) handfull of discourse, is deciphered, not what any personally is, but what any personally may be; to the intent, that by the view of others wounds we might provide playsters and cures for our owne, if occasion impose them. It is true, that all men are not borne in one, the same, or the like puritie of qualitie or condition; for in some custome is so become another nature, that reason is not the mistresse, but the seruant; not the directresse, but the foyle to their passions. Folly is a saleable merchandise, whose factour, youth, is not so allowedly profest in young men, as pleasure in men of any age: yet are the ruines, the calamities, the wofull experiences of sundrie presidents and samplars of indiscretion and weakenesse (euen in noted, and sometimes in great ones) so apparent, so daily, that no antidote the infection, disease, leprosie of so increasing an euill, can be reputed superfluous. For my part, I ingeniously acknowledge, that hitherto (however the course hath proued a barre to my thrift yet) I neuer fawned vpon any man's fortunes, whose person and merit I preferred not. Neither hath any courtship of applause set me in a higher straine, a higher pinnacle of opinion, then severest approbation might make warrantable. Howbeit, euen in these few lines that follow, my ayme hath not beene so grossely levelled, that I meant to chuse euery reader for my patron ; considering that none can challenge any interest herein from me (vnlesse he challenge it by way of an usurped impropriation) whom I myselfe doe not, out of some certaine knowledge and allowance of desert, as it were poynt out and at with my finger, and confesse that *Hic est*, it is this one, and onely. By which marke I can deny no man (not guiltie to himselfe of a selfe-unworthinesse) to call it his owne ; at least, none of those who freely returne the defects to their proper owner, and the benefit (if any may be) of this little worke to their owne use and themselues. So much, it is to bee presumed, the verie taliarie law may require, and obtaine. In all things, no one thing can more requisitely be obserued to be practised then the golden meane ; The exemplification, whereof, howeuer, heretofore attributed, I dare not so poorely undervalue myselfe and labours, as not to call mine. But, if I should farther exceede, I might exceede that meane, which I haue endeuoured to commend. Let him that is wise, and therein noble, assume properly to himselfe this interest, that I cannot distrust the successefull acceptation, where the sacrifice is a thriftie love, the patron a great man good, (for to be truly good, is to be great) and the presentor a feodorie to such as are maisters, not more of their own fortunes, then their owne affections.

Æstatis occasum haud ægrè tulit unquam
Temperata hyems.

Io. Ford.

LINEA VITÆ:

A Line of Life.

To live, and to live well, are distinct in themselues, so pecu-
liarly as is the ACTOR and the ACTION. All men couet the
former, as if it were the totall and souereigne felicitie of a
humane condition ; and some few pursue the latter, because it
giues an eternity to their blessednesse. The difference between
these two is, life, desired for the onely benifit of liuing, feares
to dye ; for such men that so liue, when they dye, both dye
finally, and dye all. But a good life aymes at another mark ;
for such men as indeauour to liue well, liue with an expectation
of death ; and they, when they dye, dye to liue, and liue for
euer. In this respect hath death (being the parting of a precious ghest from a ruinous inne, the soule from the bodie)
beene by the ancients styled a hauen of safetie, a finishing of
pilgrimages, a resting from trauaile, a passage to glorie. Everie
man that most shuns it (and he most shunnes it that most
feares it) runnes, notwithstanding, wilfully to meet it, euen
then posting to it when hee abhorres it ; for (the comparison
is liuely and remarkeable) as he who in a shippe directs his
course to some port ; whether he stand, walk, reuell, lie downe,
or any way dispose himself, is, notwithstanding, alwaies driuen
on to the period of his voyage ; so in this ship of our mortalitie, howsoeuer wee limit our courses, or are suited in any
fortune of prosperitie, or lownesse in this great sea of the world,
yet by the violence and perpetuall motion of time are we com-
peld to pace onward to the last and long home of our graues,
and then the victorie of life is concluded in the victory of our
ends.

It is granted in *philosophie* that *action* is the crowne of vertue. It cannot in *reason* (the light of philosophie) be denied that *perseuerance* is the crowne of action : and then *diuinitie,* the Queene of Nature, will confirme that *sufferance* is the crowne of perseuerance. For to be vertuous without the testimonie of imployment is as a rich minerall in the heart of the earth, un-useful, because unknowne ; yet to bee vertuously imployed, and not to continue, is like a swift runner for a prize, who can with ease gain it from others, but slothfully sitteth downe in the middle way : but to perseuere in well-doing without a sence of a dutie, only with hope of reward, is like an Indian dromedarie, that gallops to his common inne, prickt on-wardes with the desire of prouender. *It is beast-like not to differ from beasts, aswell in the abuse of reason, as it would bee in the defect.*

ACTION, PERSEVERANCE IN ACTION, SUFFERANCE IN PERSEVERANCE, are the three golden linkes that furnish vp the richest chain wherewith a good man can bee adorned. They are a tripartite counterpawne, wherby wee hold the possession of life, whose charter, or poll-deed, (as they terme it) are youth till twentie, manhood till fortie, olde age till our end. And hee who beginnes not in the spring of his minoritie to bud forth fruits of vertuous hopes, or hopefull deserts, which may ripen in the summer of confirmed manhood, rarely or neuer yeelds the crop of a plentifull memory in his age, but preuents the winter of his last houre, in the barren autume of his worst houre, by making an euen reckoning with time misspent, dying without any issue to inherit his remembrance or commendation.

Here is, then, a preparation made to the ground-worke and foundation wheron the structure and faire building of a minde nobly furnisht must stand ; which for the perpetuitie and glorie of so lasting a monument, cannot altogether unfitly bee applyed to a LINE OF LIFE : for whosoeuer shall leuell and square his whole course by this just proportion, shall (as by a line) bee led not only to unwinde himselfe from out the labyrinth and maze of this naturall and troublesome race of frailtie, but to flie up in the middle path, the *via lactea* of immortalitie in his name on earth, to the throne of life, and perfection in his whole man, and to an immortalitie that cannot bee changed.

Deceiuing and deceiuable *Palmesters*, who will undertake by the view of the hand to bee as expert in fortelling the course of life to come to others, as they are ignorant of their owne in themselues, haue framed and found out three chiefe lines in the hand, wherby to diuine future euents : — *the line of life, the middle naturall line, and the table line.* According to the fresh colour or palenes, length or shortnesse, bredth or narrownesse, straitnesse, or obliquitie, continuance, or intermission, of either of these, they presume to censure the manners, the infirmities, the qualities, the verie power of life or death of the person : but the *line of life* is the eminent mark they must be directed by to the perfection of their master-piece. All which are as far from truth as wonder ; onely it is true, and wonderfull, that any ignorance can be so deluded. Another *line of life* is the most certaine and infallible rule which wee, as we are men, and more then men, Christians, and more then Christians, the image of our Maker, must take our leuel by. Neither is judgement to be given by the ordinary lineaments of the furniture of nature, but by the noble indowments of the mind ; whose ornaments or ruines are then most apparently goodly, or miserable, when as the actions we do are the evidences of a primitiue puritie, or a deriuatiue deprauation. Here is a great labour to indure, a great strength in that labour to conquer, a great resolution in that strength to triumph, requisite before wee can climbe the almost impregnable and inaccessible toppe of glorie ; which they that haue attempted haue found, and they that haue found, haue enjoyed to their own happinis, and wonder of imitation.

RESOLUTION is the plotter and the Actor : nay, it is both the plot, and the act it selfe that must prompt vs how to doe, aswell as it must point us out what to doe, before wee can as much as take into the hands of our purposed constancie this *line*, which must direct us to life, and make us to live.

Whatsoeuer, therefore, in those briefe ensuing collections is inserted to patterne and personate an excellent man, must be concluded and understood, for method's sake, in this one onely attribute, RESOLUTION ; for by it are exemplified the perfections of the minde, consisting in the whole furniture of an enriched soule ; and to it are referred the noblest actions, which are the externall arguments and proofes of the treasure within. For, as it is a state maxime in pollicie, that *force abroad in warre is of no force, but rather rashnesse then souldierie, vnlesse there be counsell peaceably at home to direct for expedition*, so are all actions of resolution, in the œconomie, and household gouernment of a man's owne particular priuate wealth, but shining follies, vnlesse there bee a consultation first held within him, for determining the commoditie, the conveniencie and commendation of such actions, aswell in doing, as when they are done.

Order, in euerie taske, is for conceipte easiest, for demonstration playnest, for imitation surest. Let vs, then, take into our consideration this *Line of Life*, and trace the way wherein wee are to trauaill, keeping our eye on the compasse, whereby we may runne to the Paradise of memorable happinesse. And first it is to be obserued, that *Resolution* hath three branches. The one concerns a man's owne particular person for the carriage of himselfe in his proper dutie ; and such an one is knowne by none other note, then in beeing A MAN. Another concernes a man's imployment in affaires for his country, prince, and common-wealth ; and such a one is knowne by the generall name of A PUBLIKE MAN. The last concernes a man's voluntarie traffique in ciuill causes, without the imposition of authoritie, only vrged on to performe the offices of a friend, as a priuate statist to seuerall ends, all tending to goodnes and vertue ; and such a one is euer to be call'd a GOOD MAN. In euerie one of those there is a plentifull imployment, presenting it selfe to the liberall choyce for ennobling themselues with publique honors, or gayning them the truest honour, *a deserued fame*, which is one (if worthie) of the best and highest rewards of vertue.

Superfluous it were, and unnecessarie, to enter into the contentious lists of diuided philosophers, or vnreconciled schoolemen, for the absolute and punctuall definition of man ; since it sufficeth vs to be assured that he is mainely, and yet pithily, distinguisht from all other created substances in the only possession of a *reasonoble soule.* This royall prerogatiue alone poynts him to be noblest of creatures ; and, to speak truth, in an assertion not to be gain-said, he containes the summary of all the *great world* in the *little world* of himselfe. As, then, the fabricke of the globe of the earth would of necessitie runne to the confusion out of which it was first refined, if there were not a great and watchfull prouidence, to measure it in the just ballance of preseruing and sustayning ; so, consequently, without question, the frame of our humane composition must preposterously sinke vnder its burthen, if warre and prudent direction, as well in manners as in deedes, restraine it not from the dissolution and wracke, the procliuitie of corrupted nature doth hourely slide into.

Of the first, a man

A man's minde is the man himselfe, (said the Romane orator) and the chiefest of the Grecian naturalists was confident to averre, that the *temperature of the minde followed the temperature of the body.* It were a lesson worthie to be cond, if eyther of those rules may be positiuely receiued ; for out of the first, as any man feeles his inclinations and affections, thereafter let him judge himselfe to bee such a man : out of the latter it may be gathered, how easie it were for euerie man to be his owne schoole-master, in the conformation, or reformation of his life, without other tutour then himselfe.

Cicero Arist.

Socrates his speech of the use of mirrours or looking glasses concludes whatsoeuer can bee ranged in many wordes of this subject, and is, therefore, notoriously vsefull, and vsefully

E

notable. When thou viewest thy selfe in a mirrour, (said that wise man) surveyest thy complexion, thy proportion, if thy face be more faire, louely, and sweeter than others, thy bodie straighter, thy lineaments perfecter, consider how much more thou art bound by that to match those blessings of nature with the accomplishment of more noble qualities then others of a courser mould. If, on the other side, thou perceiue thy face deformed, thy body crooked, thy outward constitution vnsightly or mis-shapen, by so much the more hast thou reason to liue a good life, that thereby concord of vertuous conditions may supply the defects of nature, and make thee more beautifull inwardly to the eye of judgement, then outwardly thou couldst haue beene to the eyes of popular delight.

In short, to be a *man*, the first branch of resolution is to know, feele, and moderate affections, which, like traitors and disturbers of peace, rise vp to alter, and quite change the lawes of reason, by working in the feeble, and oftentimes the sounder parts, an innovation of folly. Hee can seldome be a flourishing member of a bodie politique, and so a *publique deseruing man*; but more rarely, scantly euer, a reconciler of divisions, and so a ciuill *good man* for others, that begins not betimes to discharge his owne dutie to himselfe. The old proverbe was, (and it is lamentable to speake with truth, and say it is) that *a man is a beast to a man*; but it must be of necessitie granted, when a man to himselfe is a *monster*, or, more proverbially, *a devill*.

Homo homini lupus

It is said of CAIVS CVRIO, that hee was a man most *wittily wicked*, and most *singularly eloquent* in mischiefe against the common-wealth. What rarities were here lost! (like a diamond set in a rushen ring.) How much better had it been for him to haue had a *duller braine*, if better imployed, and a *slower tongue*, if auaileable for the publique good? Euery man should, in his owne person, endeuour and striue to be like *Catoes Orator, a good man; and expert in pleading*. First *good*, then *expert*; for of so much richer price is *vertue* than *art*: *art*, without *vertue*, being like the *Cantharides*, whose wings

Velleius Paterc, lib. 2

Fabius Orat. lib. 12, cap. 1
Plin. lib. 11, cap. 35

puld off, they haue prettie colours to please the eye, but poisonous substances to be receiued into the stomack. How easie it is to guild a rotten post, to paint a sepulcher, to varnish an ill meaning, is soone resolued : many men can *speake well*, few men will *doe well ;* the reason for that we covet to be thought what wee are not, and yet continue to be what wee are ashamed to be thought.

The excellency of goodnesse is apparent mainly in this one poynt, that euen those who least practise it in outward appearance cunningly labour to make it the marke whereto all their actions (how foule soever in the issue) leuell at. It was truely obserued by a graue author, that there was neuer any publique mischiefe attempted in a state by euen atheists, or very incarnate deuils, but religion was their colour to effect it ; at least a shew of some false zeale in as false a worship : for there must be an intention of vertue in the worst actions, otherwise they could neuer haue passage by any publique approbation ; insomuch, that hypocrisie is reputed the surest and the safest ground of pollicie.

By this appeareth the richnesse of vertue, that euen such as most oppose it must, and are compelled to acknowledge it for best. In like manner, euery man, in his particular to distinguish his actions, is, in his knowledge, guiltie and conscious of what he doth or should doe. We were not borne to feed, sleepe, and spinne out our webbe of life in the delicate softnesse of vanitie or sloath ; wee were not borne to traffique in follies, and to make merchandize of our sensualities ; wee were not borne to reuel in the apishnesse of ridiculous expence of time ; wee were not borne to be panders to that great whore of a declyning reason, *bewitching pleasure ;* we were not borne to laugh at our owne securitie, but to bewayle it ; we were not borne to liue for our selues, but to our selues ; as we were not, on the other side, borne to dye to our selues, but for our selues. We must learne to rejoyce in true goodnesse, not vain delights ; for, as we cannot judge him to haue a light heart alwaies that

E 2

somtimes laughes (for euen in laughter there is a sadnesse), so wee must not imitate, by any outward demeanor, to bewray the minoritie of our resolution, except we would be as childish in understanding as in action.

What infinite inticers hath a man, as he is a meere man, to withdraw him from an erected heart ! As the temptation of a reputed beautie, the invitement of a presented honour, the be-witching of an inforced wealth, the lethargie and disease of an infectious court-grace ; yet all, and euerie one of these (with what other appendances soeuer belonging vnto them) are, if not wisely made vse of, but glorious snares, dangerous baites, golden poysons, dreaming distructions, snares to intrappe the mightineese of constancie, baites to deceiue the constancie of manhood, poysons to corrupt the manhood of resolution, destruction to quite cast away the resolution of a just desert.

Now, for a man's carriage in his particular dutie, what can hee determine of, since he hath not more himselfe, and his own affections to assault and batter his resolution in the path of vertue, then a world of presidents, of partners, of helpers, to perswade and draw him on to the full measure of an vnworthy life ? It is a labor wel worthie a chronicle (and chronicled will bee in a perpetuall memorie) to withstand the seuere assault of folly, pressing on with so infinite an armie of followers, and admirers, as shee is accompanyed with. What can one *priuate man* do against such a multitude of temptations ? Either hee must consent to doe as they doe, or dissent and hate them : if consent, hee is mischievous with many ; if dissent, vertuous by himselfe ; and the last is without controversie the best, since neuer to haue seene euill is no praise to well doing ; but where the actours of mischiefe are a nation, there, and amongst them, to liue well is a crowne of immortal commendation.

A golden axiome there was registred amongst the ciuilians in the daies of *Justinian: that it was not convenient for any man to pry and looke after what was done at Rome, but to examine justly what ought there to bee done. Rome* was then the mart of the world : all sorts of euery people came thither, from thence to receiue the oracles of life (as they might bee termed) ; yet doth it not follow that any one man, with the multitude, should runne to *Rome* to sucke the infection of dissolute intemperature. *Vanity* most commonly rides coach't in the high way, the beaten way, the common way ; but *Vertue and Moderation* walkes alone. It may be said, what profit can redound, what commendation, what reward, for one man to be singular against many ? O ! the profit is infinite, the commendation memorable, the reward immortall. It is true, the olde Greeke prouerbe concluded that *one man was no man* ; yet, with their most approued authours, by the verie word MANY were the worst sort of people vnderstood ; and by FEW, the best. For certainely there is not any allurement could lull men in the trust of their misdeeds, so much as those two pestilent yoke-fellowes and twinnes of confusion, *the multitude of offenders, and the libertie of offending.* They are both examples and schoole-masters, to teach euen the very ignorant (whose simplicitie else might be their excuse) to do what (if others did not) they might accidentally slide into, but not so eagerly pursue.

To conclude this point, it may somewhat too truly be said, though not by way of discouragement, yet of caveat, what by the proclivitie and pronenesse of our frailtie is warrantable, *Let no man bee too confident of his owne merit ; the best doe erre. Let no man relye too much on his owne judgement ; the wisest are deceiued.* Yet, let euery man so conceiue of himselfe, that he may indeuour to bee such a one, as distrust shal not make him carelesse, or confidence secure.

It followes, that the very consideration of being men should somwhat rectifie our crooked inclinations, and ennoble our actions, to keepe vs worthy of the priuiledge wee haue aboue beasts : otherwise, only to be a man in substance and name is no more glorie, then to bee knowne and distinguished from a very beast in nature.

Presidents from antiquitie may plentifully be borrowed, to

e

set before vs what some men haue beene, not as they were commanders, or employed for the commonwealth, but as they were commanders of their owne infirmities, and employed for the commonwealth of their own particular persons. *Epaminondos*, amongst the *Thebanes*, is worthy of note and memorie, euen to our ages and those that shall succeed vs. Hee (as the philosopher recordeth) chose rather to bee moderate alone, then madde with the multitude; chusing at all times to consult with himselfe in excellent things, not with his countrymen to giue lust, dalliance, effeminate softnes, a regiment in the kingdome of his thoughts; no, not of his thoughts, much lesse of his actions. *Phocion*, among the *Athenians*, *Brutus*, among the *Romanes*, are for their particular cariage of themselues, as they were only men, well worthy of all remembrance: and the sententious Seneca is bold to say, that all ages will euer hatch and bring forth many such as *Clodius* (a man bent to mischiefe), but rarely any age another *Cato*, a man so sincere, so free from corruption, and so severe a censurer of himselfe.

But what need we to search histories of other times, or the deserts of another nation, when, in our owne land, in our owne dayes, wee might easily patterne what a man should bee or not bee, by what others haue bin? Among many, two of late times are justly examined; not as they were different in fortune, in yeares, in degree, but as they differed in the use of the gifts of their mind. The first was JOHN, the last and yongest Lord HARRINGTON, whose rare and admirable course of life (not as he was a nobleman, for then indeed it were miraculous, but as a man) deserues all prayse, and imitation from all. Of whome it may without flatterie, (for what benefit can accrue to flatter the dead?) or affection bee said, that he, amongst a world of men, attayned, euen in his youth, not only to grauitie in his behauiour, to wisedome in his vnderstanding, to ripenesse in his carriage, to discretion in his discourse, but to perfection

Plutarch in Apotheg.

Cicero de leg. lib. 3

Epist. 98

in his action : a man wel-deserving even the testimonie of a religious learned diuine.

But for that his owne merit is his best commendation, and questionlesse his surest reward for morall gifts, let him rest in his peace, whilest the next is to bee obserued.

SIR WALTER RAULEIGH may be a second president ; a man known, and wel-deserving to be knowne ; a man endued not with common endowments, being stored with the best of Nature's furniture, taught much by much experience, experienc'd in both fortunes so feelingly and apparently that it may truly bee controuerted whether hee were more happie or miserable ; yet, beholde in him the strange character of a *meere man*, a man subject to as many changes of *resolution*, as resolute to bee the instrument of change : *politique*, and yet in *policie* so unstedie, that his too much apprehension was the foile of his judgement. *For what man soeuer leaues*

*　　　　*　　　　*　　　　*　　　　*

*　　　　*　　　　*　　　　*　　　　*

*　　　　*　　　　*　　　　*　　　　*

hend all what the former discourse hath amplified ; namely, that *the only felicitie of a good life depends in doing all things* Seneca Epist. *freely, by beeing content with what wee haue (for wee speake of a* [128] *morall man). This is to remember that we are mortal, that our dayes passe on, and our life slides away without recoverie.*

Great is the taske, the labour painfull, the discharge full of Of the second danger, and the dangers full of enuy, that he must of necessitie branch, a pub- vndergoe, that, like a blaze upon a mountain, stands neerest in like man grace to his prince : or, like a vigilant-sentinell in a watch-tower, busies and weakens his owne naturall and vitall spirits, to administer equalitie and iustice to all, according to the requisition of his office.

It is lamentable, and much to bee pittyed, when places of authority in a commonwealth are disposed of to some, whose vnworthinesse, or disabilitie, brings a scandall, a scorne, and a reproch to both the place and the minister.

Plato, 3, 6;
& 12 de leg.
& 7 de Repub.
Arist. 7 ; &
6 Pol.
Isocrat. in
Pan.

The best law-makers amongst the ancients were so curious in their choice of men in office in the commonwealth, that precisely and peremptorily they reputed that STATE plagued, whipped, tormented, wounded, yea, wounded to death, where the subordinate gouernours were not as well vnblemished in their liues and actions, as in their names and reputation.

A PUBLIKE MAN hath not more neede to be *bonus ciuis*, a good *statist*, then *bonus vir*, good in himselfe : a very faire and large *line* is limmed out to square by it a direct path that leades to a vertuous name, if a man acquite himselfe nobly, justly, and wisely, in well steering the helme of state that he sits at ; otherwise, his honours are but a burthen, his height a curse, his fauours a destruction, his life a death, and his death a misery ; a misery in respect of his after defamation, as well as of his after accompt.

Far from the present purpose it is to dive into the depth of *policie*, or to set downe any positiue rules what a right *states-man* should be ; for that were with *Phormio*, the philosopher, to read a Lecture of souldierie to *Hannibal*, the most cunningest warriour of his time : and, consequently, as *Phormio* was by *Hannibal* to be justly laughed at, so as well might *Seneca* haue written to *Nero* the art of crueltie, or *Cicero* to his brother *Quintus* the commendation of anger. The summe of these briefe collections is intended to recreate the minde ; not to in-forme knowledge in practice, but to conforme practice to know-ledge. Whereto no indeavor can bee found more requisite, more availeable then an vndeceiuing lesson of an impartiall ob-seruation ; wherin if our studies erre not with many, and those approued, thus we haue obserued.

Two sorts of publike men

First, of publique men there are two generall sorts : the one, such as by speciall fauour of their prince (which fauour cannot ordinarily be conferred without some mayne, and euident note of desert) haue been raised to a supereminent ranck of honour and so by degrees (as it for the most part alwayes happens) to speciall places of weightie imployment in the common wealth.

The other sort are such as the prince according to his judgement
hath, out of their owne sufficiencie, aduaunced to particular
offices, whether for administration of justice, for execution of
law, for necessitie of seruice, and the like ; being, according to
their education and studie, enabled for the discharge of those
places of authoritie : and *these two* are the onely chiefe and
principall members of imploiment, under that head, of whose
politike bodie they are the most usefull and stirring members.

Against both those publique persons there are *two capitall
and deadly opposites* (if it were possible) to becharme their
resolutions, and blot out their name from the LINE OF LIFE, by
which they should be led to the endlesse immortalitie of an
immortalitie, in an euer-flourishing commendation. *The first*
are poysoners of vertue, the betrayers of goodnesse, the bloud-
suckers of innocencie : *the latter*, the close deaths-men of
merit, the plotters against honestie, and the executioners of
honors. They are in two words discovered, *blandientes &
sævientes*, flatterers, and privie murtherers. It is a disputable
question, and well worthie a canvase and discussion in the
schools, to decide which of the two doe the greatest injurie to
noble personages. How be it, most apparent it is, that enuie,
the inseparable companion that accompanies the vertuous,
doeth not worke more mischiefe for the finall ouerthrow of a
noble and deseruing man, then flattery doth, for driuing that
noble and deseruing man into the snares of enuie. No man
can be, or should be reputed a god ; and then how easie it is
for any man of the choycest temper, of the soundest apprehension, of the gracefullest education, of the sincerest austeritie of
life, how easie it is for him to fall into many errours, into
many unbecomming follies, into many passions, and affections :
his onely being *a man* is both sufficient proofe, and yet sufficient excuse. The eloquentest and grauest diuine of all the Augustine.
ancients confest, out of his owne experience, *non est mihi
vicinior hostis memet ipso ;* that he had not a more neere
enemie to him then himselfe : for he that hath about him his

frailtie to corrupt him, a world to besot him, an aduersarie to
terrifie him, and, lastly, a death to devoure him, how should
hee but bee inveigled with the inticements of the *two first*, and
so consequently consent to the vnsteadinesse of his temptation,
before he be drawne to a serious consideration of the daunger of
the *two last ?*—especially as we are men, being not onely subiect to the lapses and vanities of men, but as we are eminent
men, in grace and fauour, in prioritie of titles, of place, and of
command ; having men to sooth us up in the maintenance and
countenancing of those euils, which else doubtlesse could not,
at one time or other, but appeare before us in their own ugli-
nesse and deformitie.

A flatterer is the onely pestilent bawd to great mens shames,
the nurse to their wantonnesse, the fuell to their lusts ; and,
with his poyson of artificiall villanie, most times doth set an
edge vnto ryot, which otherwise would be blunted, and rebated,
in the detestation of their own violent posting to a violent confusion. Not vnwisely did a wise man compare a *flattering language*
to a *silken halter*, which is *soft* because *silken*, but strangling because a halter. The words wherewith those *panders of vice* doe
perswade are not so louely, as the matters they dawbe ouer with
their adulations are abhominable. That is a bitter sweetnesse,
which is onely delicious to the pallate, and to the stomacke
deadly. It is reported, that all beasts are wonderfully delighted
with the sent of the breath of the panther, a beast fierce and
cruell by nature, but that they are else affrighted with the
sternesse of his lookes : for which cause the panther, when he
hunts his prey, hiding his grimme visage, with the sweetnesse
of his breath allures the other beastes vnto him, who, being
come within his reach, hee rends and cruelly doth dilaniate
them. Even so, those patrons and *minions of false pleasures,
the flatterers,* that they may prey vpon the credulitie of the
abused GREAT ONES, imitate the panthers, extenuating, and,
as much as in them lyes, hiding the grossnesse, the vglinesse,
the deformitie of those follyes they perswade vnto ; and with

Diog, Laert.
in vita Diog.

Plin. hist. lib.
8. cap. 17

a false glosse varnishing and setting out the paradise of vncon-
trolled pleasures, to the ruine, oftimes, of the informed, and
glorie of their owne pietie.

Is such a MIGHTIE MAN inticed to ouer-rule his reason, nay,
ouer-beare it, by giuing scope to his licentious eye, first to see,
then to delight in—lastly to couet a chaste beauty ? Alasse !
how many swarms of dependants, being creatures to his
greatnesse, will not onely tell him, mocke him, and harden
him in a readie and pregnant deceipt, that loue is courtly, and
women were in their creation ordained to be wooed, and to be
won, but also what numbers of them will thrust themselues
into imploiments and seruile action, to affect the lewdnesse of
desire, to corrupt with promises, with guifts, with perswasions,
with threatnings, with entreaties, to force a rape on vertue, and
adulterate the chaste bosome of spotlesse simplicitie. A folly
is committed ; how sleight are they ready to prove it, how
sedulous to sleighten, how damnably disposed to make it
nothing ! insomuch as those vipers of humanitie are fitly to be
termed the *man's whore,* and the *woman's knaue.* Is such a
mightie one affected to such a suite, as the graunt and possession of it will draw a curse vpon his head by a generall voyce
of a generall smarte, and detriment, to the commonwealth ?
How suddenly will those wilde beasts labour to assure him,
that the multitudes loue is wonne by keeping them in awe, not
by giuing way to their giddinesse by any affabilitie ! Will
another aduance an vnworthy *court-ape,* and oppresse a desertfull hope ? It were too tedious to recite what incessant appro-
bations will bee repeated by these *Anthropophagi,* those men-
eaters to make a *golden calfe* an idoll, and a *neglected merite* a
laughter. That such a kinde of monsters may appeare in their
likenesse as monstrous as in effect they are, it is worthie
obseruation to see how, when any man, who, whiles hee stood
chiefe in the prince's fauour, they honoured as an earthly god,
yet, being declyned from his prince's estimation, it is worthie
to be noted how speedily, how swiftly, how maliciously those

cankers of a state will not onely fall off, will not onely dispise, will not onely deride, but also oppose themselues against the partie distasted.

As many subtill practizers of infamie haue other subordinate ministers of publique office and imployment in a common-wealth to betray them to their ruine, yet ever and anon they, like inchanted glasses, set them on fire with the false light of concealement and extenuation. Let it be spoken with some authority, borrowed from experience of the elder times, that men in high places are like some hopelesse marriners, set to sea in a leaking vessel : there is no safetie, no securitie, no com-fort, no content in greatnesse, vnlesse it be most constantly armed in the defensive armor of a selfe-worthie resolution ; especially when their places they hold are hourely subject to innouation, as their names (if they prevent not their dangers by leauing them and their liues at once) are to reproach, and the libertie of malice.

Flatterie to either publique persons is not more inductious on the one side, then enuie on the other is vigilant. Great men are by great men (not good men by good men) narrowly sifted ; their liues, their actions, their demeanors examined, for that their places and honours are hunted after, as the *beazar* for his preservatiues ; and then the least blemish, the least slide, the least error, the least offence is exasperated, made capitall : the dangers ensuing euer prooue (like the wound of an enemie's sword) mortall, and many times deadly. Now, in this case, when the eye of judgement is awakened, flatterie is discouered to be but an inmate to *envie ;* an inmate, at least, consulting together, though not dwelling together, the one being catarer to the other's bloodie banquet : and some wise men haue been perswaded that the pestilence, the rigour of law, famine, sicknes, or war, haue not devour'd more great ones then *flatterie and envie.*

Much amisse, and from the purpose, it cannot bee to giue instance in three publike presidents of three famous nations, all chancing within the compasse of twentie yeares. In *England*, not long agoe, a man supereminent in honours, desertfull in many services, indeared to a vertuous and a wise queene, ELIZABETH of glorious memorie, and eternall happinesse ; a man, too, publikely beloued, and too confident of the loue he held, ROBERT EARLE OF ESSEX, and Earle Marshall of the kingdome ; he, euen he, that was thought too high to fall, and too fixed to be removed, in a verie handfull of time felt the miserie of greatnesse, by relying on such as flattered and envyed his greatnesse. His end was their end ; and the execution of law is a witnesse in him to posteritie, how a publike person is not at any time longer happie, then hee preserues his happinesse with a resolution that depends vpon the guard of innocencie and goodnes.

CHARLES DUKE OF BYRON, in *France*, not long after him, ranne the same fate ; a prince that was reputed the inuincible fortresse to his king and countrey ; great in desert, and too great in his greatnesse. Not managing the fiery chariot of his, guiding the sunne of that climate, with moderation, gave testimonie, by an imposed and inexpected end, how a publike man in authoritie sits but in commission on his own delinquencie, longer then *resolution* in noble actions leuels at the immortalite of *A Line of Life*.

Lastly, SIR JOHN VANOLDEN BARNEVELT, in the Netherlands, (whose ashes are scarce yet colde) is, and will bee, a liuely president of the mutabilitie of greatnesse. Hee was the only one that traffiqued in the counsels of foreine princes, had factors in all courts, intelligencers amongst all Christian nations ; stood as the ORACLE of the prouinces, and was even the moderator of policies of all sorts ; was reputed to bee second to none on earth for soundnesse of designes ; was indeed his countreyes both mynion, mirror, and wonder : yet, enforcing his publike authoritie too much to bee seruant to his priuate ambition, hee left the tongue of *justice* to proclayme, that *long life* and a *peacefull death* are not granted or held by the charter of honours, except vertuous RESOLUTION renew the patent, at a daily expence of proficiencie in goodnesse.

Others, fresh in memorie, might bee inserted, but these are yet bleeding in the wounds which they haue giuen themselues ; and some now liuing to this day, who both haue had, and doe enjoy, as great honours, and are therefore as incident to as many wofull changes, but that they wisely provide to proppe their greatnesse with many greater deserts.

Here is in text letters layd before us the hazard, perill, and casuality of A PVBLIKE MAN ; the possibilitie what miserie, calamity, ruine, greatnesse, and popularitie may winde him into. Heere is decyphered the unavoydable and incessant per-secutors of their honours and joyes, *flatterie and envie, two ancient courtiers.* It comes now to conclusion, that it cannot be denyed but those *publike men* haue (notwithstanding these) chiefe and immediate meanes in their owne powers, if they well and nobly order their courses to make their countrey their debtors, and to enroll their names in the glorious register of an euer-memorable glorie ; especially if they be not too partially doting on euery commendable vertue, which in priuate men is reputed, as it is, a vertue, but in them miracle. Certainly (without disparagement to desert in great men) there are many particular persons fit for publike imployments, whose ablenesse and sufficiencie is no way inferior to the prayses of the mightiest, but that they are clouded in their lownesse, and obscured in their priuatenesse, but else would, and could, giue testimony to the world, that all fulnesse and perfection is not confined to eminence and authoritie.

A PVBLIKE MAN, therefore, shunning the adulation of a parasite, (which hee may easily discouer, if hee wisely examine his merit with their hyperbolical insinuations) then keeping an euen course in the processe of lawfull and just actions, auoyd-ing the toyles, snares, and trappes of the enuious, cannot chuse in his own lifetime but build a monument, to which the triumph and trophies of his memorie shall giue a longer life then the

perpetuitie of stone, marble, or brasse, can preserue. Otherwise, if they stand not on the guard of their owne pietie and
wisedome, they will vpon trifles, sometime or other, bee quar-
relled against and evicted.   Neyther may they imagine that
any one taint (howsoeuer they would bee contented to winke
at it in themselues, supposing it to be (as perhaps it is) little,
and not worthy reprehension) can escape vnespyed ; for the
morall of the poet's fiction is a goodly lesson for their in-
struction.   It is said that *Thetis*, the mother of *Achilles*, drencht
him, being an infant, in the *Stygian* waters, that thereby his
whole bodie might bee made invulnerable : but see the seueritie
of Fate ; for in that part of the heele that his mother held him
by was hee shot by the arrow of *Paris*, of which wound he
dyed.   In like ease, may euery statesman bee like *Achilles* in
the generall body of his actions, impassible and secure from
any assault of wilfull and grosse enormitie, yet, if he giue
way to *but one* handfull (as it may be termed) of folly, not
becomming the grauity and greatnes of his calling, hee shall
soone meete with some watchfull *Paris*, some industrious flatterer, or ouer-busie enuious competitour, that will take aduan-
tage of his weaknesse, and wound his infirmitie to the ruin of
his honours, if not to the jeopardy of his life.

The period of all shal be knit vp with the aduise of a famous
learned [man] and philosopher ; and, as he wrote to his familiar Sen. Epi. 23
friend, let vs transcribe to men in authoritie :—*Let a publike*
man rejoyce in the true pleasures of a constant resolution, not in
the deceiuable pleasures of vanitie and fondnesse. By a good
conscience, honest counsells, and just actions, the true good is
acquired : other momentany delights only supple the forehead, not
unburthen and solace the heart. They are nothing, alasse ! they
are nothing : it is the minde must be well disposed, it is the minde
must bee confident ; it is the mind, aboue all things, must be
rectified, and the true comfort is not easily attayned, and yet with
more difficulty retayned.   But hee, he who directs all his whole
priuate life in honourable projections, cannot any way misse

our LINE OF LIFE, which points at the immortalitie of a vertuous name, by profitably discharging the burthen of such imployments as are vsually imposed vpon those, whom their callings haue entitled *publike men*.

Of the 3 branch, a good man.

A GOOD MAN is the last branch of *resolution*, and by him is meant (as is said before) such a man as doth (beside the care he hath of himselfe in particular) attend all his drifts and actions to bee a seruant for others, for the good of others, as if it were his owne.   School-boyes, newly trayned vp in the principles of grammer, can resolue what a good man is, or who ?   Who ? *Qui consulta patrum, qui leges juraque servat*.   Such a one as not indeed singly obserues what he should doe, but doth euen that which hee obserues hee should doe.   This man not only liues, but liues well, remembring alwayes the old adage, that God is there warder of aduerbes, not of nownes.   His intents are without the hypocrisie of applause, his deedes without the mercenary expectation of reward ; the issue of both is, all his workes are crown'd in themselues, and yet crowne not him, for that hee loues *vertue* for it selfe.   *This man* neuer flatters folly in greatnesse, but rather pitties ; and, in pitie, strives to redresse the greatnesse of folly.   *This man* neuer envies the eminence of Authoritie, nor feares the enuious : his reprehensions are balms, his prayses glories; and he is as thankfull to be rebuked, as to bee cherished.   From such *a man* all things are to be gratefully accepted : his desire to doe good to all hath not a like successe to all (notwithstanding in him *to will* is commendable, and not to be able *to doe* pardonable) : for it is not only the propertie of true vertue, but also of true friendship, as well to admonish as to bee admonished ; for amongst *good men* those things are euer well taken that are well meant.   Yet euen *this man* (that vncompeld, vnrequired, not exacted) interposes himselfe, to set at vnitie the disorders of others not so inclinable to goodnesse, is not free from enmity with those who, in a general care, he labours to deserue as friends.   The reason *flattery procures friends, truth hatred* — how !   Truth

hatred? Yes, for from truth is hatred borne, which is the Cicero de Amicit.
poyson of friendship, as Lælius wel obserued. But what
ensues? Hee whose eares are so fortified and barrocaded
against the admitment of truth, that from his friend he wil
not heare the truth, this man's safetie is desperat. Wherfore,
if any one will only relish *words of downe and honey*, as if wee
loued to speake nothing but *pure roses* (as the prouerbe is), let
such a one learn from the skilfull artists of nature, that the bees Plin. hist. lib. 11. Cap. 6
doe anoynt their hiues with the juyce of the bitterest weeds,
against the greedinesse of other beasts. Let him learne from
the skilfullest phisicians, that the healthfullest medicines smart
most in the wound. Let him learne from the prince of philo- Arist. Eth. lib. 3
sophie, that anger was giuen to men by nature (as hee writes)
as a whetstone of valour ; and then he cannot but consider, that
any paines which a *good man* undergoes for reconciliation, be
they either by way of admonition, or reprehension, tend both to
one end, and that hee may make all like vnto himselfe, that
is, *good men*.

This very word (GOOD) implyes a description in it selfe,
more pithy, more patheticall, then by any familiar exemplification can be made manifest : such a man as makes the
generall commoditie his particular benefit, may not vnfitly be
stiled a PRIVATE STATESMAN. His endeauours are publike, the
use publike, the profit publike, the commendation publike ; but
the person priuate, the resolution priuate, the end priuate, and
the reward peculiar.

It is impossible that the wretched and avaricious banking vp
of wealth can draw him into a conceipt, that hee can euer make
friends of mony after his death, considering that the world was
created for the use of men, and men created into the world *to
use it, not to enjoy it*. This man's bounty is giuing, not lending ;
and his giuing is free, not reserued. He cherisheth learning in
the learned, and incourageth the learned to the loue of learning
by cherishing them. He heartneth the vpright in justice, and
ratifies justice in the vpright. He helpes the distressed with

F

counsell, and approues the proceedings of wise counsellors. He is a patterne to all what they should be, as he is to himselfe what he is.

Finally, try all his desires, his actions are the seasoners of his speeches, as his profession is of his actions. Hee is a physitian to other men's affections, as to his own, by comprimitting such passions as runne into an insurrection, by strengthening such as decline, by suppling such as are inflamed, by restrayning such as would runne out, by purging such as ouerabound. His ambition climbs to none other cure then to heale the wounded, not to wound the whole ; beeing neither so vnwise to doe any thing that he ought not to doe, nor so vnhappy to doe any thing what hee does not. His singular misfortune is, that with Drusus (an excellent man) he attempts many times with a more honest and good mind, then good fortune and successe ; insomuch as it often comes to passe that other men's mischiefes are preferred before his vertues : yet still as he is *a good man ;* injuries can no more discourage him, than applause can ouer-weene him.

Euen this man hath his particular aduersaries to threaten him ; and (if it could be possible) to terrifie him, and deter him from the soliditie of his temper : *scandal* to defame him, and *imposture* to traduce him. *Flatterie* and *envie* are not a more pestilent broode, set in armes against a *publique man,* then these two miscreant monsters are against a *good man*. But is his resolution any way infracted, for that some refractaries are (like knights of the post) hired to witnesse against him ? Doubtlesse no, but much more the rather confirmed to run by a LINE OF LIFE to the *goale of life*. His owne solace is to him as an inexpugnable castle of strength against all the forcible assaults of divellish exploits, built onely vpon this foundation, that he is conscious to himselfe of an vnforced sinceritie. With the poet he can resolue : *Hic murus aheneus esto, nil conscire sibi :* his integritie to him is a brazen wall : and with the orator he assures himselfe that *nullum theatrum cirtuti majus consci-*

Velleius hist.
Rom. lib. 2

Horat. lib. 1,
Epist. 1

Cicer. quæst.
Tusc. lib. 2

entiâ : vertue hath not a more illustrious and eminent theatre to act on, then her owne conscience. Socrates (a good man, if a meere morall man may be termed so) beeing scurrilously by *Aristophanes* the poet derided before the people, and by *Anytus* and *Melytus* vnjustly accused before the iudges as a trifler, a master of follies, a corrupter of youth, a sower of impieties, answered, *If their alledged imputations be true, we will amend them ; if false, they pertaine not to us.* It was a noble constancie and resolution of a wise man, that he (inlightened with the only beames of nature) was so moderate and discreet. The good man here personated (inspired with a farre richer and diuiner knowledge then humanitie) cannot but asmuch exceede Socrates in those vertues of resolution, as Socrates did his aduersaries in modestie and moderation.

In Comœd. Νεφαλαις

Plat. apol. Socrat.

Diog. Laert. in vita Socrat

Kings and mightie monarches, as they are first movers to all subordinate ministers, of what ranke or imploiments soever, within their proper dominions, are indeed *publike persons.* But as one king traffiques with another, another, and another, either for repressing of hostilities, inlarging a confederacie, confirming an amitie, settling a peace, supplanting an heresie, and such like, not immediately concerning his owne particular, or his peoples, but for moderating the differences betweene other princes ; in this respect euen *kings and priuate men,* and so their actions belong wholly and onely to themselues, printing the royalty of their goodnes in an imorrtalitie of a vertuous and euerlasting name, by which they justly lay a claime to the style *of good men :* which attribute doth more glorifie their desert, then the mightinesse of their thrones can their glories.

In which respect our SOVERAIGNE LORD AND KING, that now is, hath worthily chronicled his grand-father's remembrance, which was (as hee best witnesseth) called *The Poore Man's King ;* a title of so inestimable a wealth, that the riches of many kingdoms are of too low and meane a value to purchase the dignitie and honour of this onely style, *The Poore Man's King.*

Βασιλ. Δωρον Lib. 2

The famous and most excellent commendation of A GOOD

MAN cannot be more expressly exemplified in any president or
myrrour by all the instances of former times, nor shall euer
(farre, farre bee servilitie or insinuation) over-paralleled by any
age succeeding, then in the person of JAMES, the king of Great
Britaine, presently here reigning ouer vs. *A good man*, so well
deseruing (from all grateful memorie) seruice and honour, that
not to doe him seruice is an ingratitude to the *greatnesse of his
goodnesse*, and not to doe him all honour an ingratitude to the
goodnesse of his greatnesse. A *good man* that, euen with his
entrance to the crowne, did not more bring *peace* to all Christian nations, yea, almost to all nations of the Westerne World,
then since the whole course of his glorious reigne hath preserued
peace amongst them. *A good man* who hath thus long sought,
as an equal and vpright moderatour, to decide, discusse, conclude, and determine all differences between his neighbouring
princes and fellowes in Europe : *a good man*, of whom it may be
verified that he is BONORUM MAXIMUS, and MAGNORUM OPTIMUS :
a good man that loues not *vertue* for the name of vertue onely,
but for the substance and realities : *a good man*, whom neither scandal can any way impeach of injustice, tyrannie, ignorance, nor imposture traduce to a neglect of merite in the
desertfull, to levitie in affections, to surquedrie in passions, to
intention of inclyning to folly, or declyning from reall worth ;
which, as an hereditarie inheritance, and a fee simple by nature and education, hee retaynes in himselfe, to the wonder and
admiration of all that may emulously imitate him, never perfectly equall him. Questionlesse, the chronicles, that shall
hereafter report the annalls of his life and actions, shall doe
infinite injuries to the incomparable monuments of his name, if
they style him, as some would wish, JAMES THE GREAT, or,
as others indevour, JAMES THE PEACEABLE, or, as not a few
hope, JAMES THE LEARNED : for to those titles haue the
Greekes in *Alexander*, the Romans in *Augustus*, the Germans
in *Charles the Fift*, the French men in *Charlemaine* and *Henrie
the Fourth*, father to their present king, attayned. But if he

shall be reported in his style to be, as in his owne worthinesse hee may justly challenge, he must then be styled, as by the approbation of all that truely know him, he is knowne to be, JAMES THE GOOD. Let the summe of this branch of *resolution*, which is indeed *corona operis*, the summe of the whole sum, bee concluded :—that *this onely patterne*, as he is onely inferior on earth to God, who is BONUM SVMMUM, the chiefe and soueraigne good, so the distinction betweene his great master and him (whose vicegerent he is) consists in this (with reverence to the divine Majestie be it spoken) that as God (whom to call good is but an improprietie of description) is not singly *bonus*, good, but *bonitas*, goodnesse, *in abstracto* (as the schoole men speake): so vnder the great KING OF KINGS this king of men is substitute to his king with this vp-shut—the one is for ever the *king of goodnesse ;* and our king on earth not onely a *good king*, but a GOOD MAN ; such a *good man* as doth himselfe run, and teacheth by his example others securely and readily to runne, by his *line of life* to the immortalitie of a vertuous name.

A priuate man, a publique man, a good man, haue beene here particularly deciphered and discoursed. It comes to conclusion, that hee who desires either in his owne person to be renowned, for the generall prosperitie of the commonwealth to be eternized, or for the communitie of his friends, or any whom he will make his friends, remembred in the diaries of posteritie, must first lay the foundation of a willingnesse, from thence proceed to a desire, from thence to a delight, from a delight to practise, from practise to a constant perseuerance in noble actions. And then such a man, howsoeuer he liue, shall neuer misse to end his dayes before his honors and the honours of his name can end, for they shal knowe no end ; and yet euen in death, and after death ouer-liue all his enemies in the immortall spring of a most glorious memorie, which is the most precious crowne and reward
of a most precious
Line of Life.

F 3

THE COROLLARIE.

In the view of the precedent argument somewhat (perhaps) too lamely hath the progresse of a man's life (in any fate) been traced, wherein still the course, like a pilot sayling for his safety and welfare, hath alwayes had an eie to the north-starre of vertue, without which men cannot but suffer shipwrack on the land, as well as mariners on the sea. Such as haue proofes in their owne persons and experiences of both fortunes haue past through their dangers of their beeing men, as they were first priuat, before they entered, and from their entrance waded into the labyrinth of greatnesse and imployment, from whence they became *publike men*. Now then somewhat boldly (yet the boldnes is a presumption of loue, not loue of presumption) may bee intimated, that howsoeuer any great or popular person (for to such doth this application properly appertaine, howbeit free from any particularity, except particularly challenged) in a peculiar examination of himselfe cannot chuse but find, that he hath encountred many oppositions of youth (euen in graue yeares) and frailtie (in graue actions.) Yet hauing at any time, by any casualtie, a happinesse (danger it selfe is a happinesse if rightly made vse of, otherwise a miserie) to account with his expence of time, he cannot, vpon indifferent and euen reckoning, instead of impayring his honours, but aduance them : he cannot, if he account faithfully, instead of making the world his confessour, but confesse his owne noblenesse ; and therevpon he will find that the toyle in common affaires is but trash and bondage, compared to the sweet repose of the minde, and the goodly contemplation of man's peace with himselfe. All glory, whether it consist of profits or preferments, is WITHOUT, and therefore makes nothing to the essence of true happinesse ; but the feeling of a resolued constancie is WITHIN, and euer keepes a feast in a man's soundest content. One pregnant and notable samplar deserues an eye of judgement to be fixed on it. *Demosthenes*, after a long gouernment at his pleasure in the common-wealth, (vpon what consideration he himselfe knew best, and states-men may easily guesse at) is reported to confesse to his friends who came to visit him, that if at the beginning *two waies* had bin proposed before him, *the one* leading to the tribunall of authoritie, *the other* to his graue, if hee could, by inspiration, haue fore-knowne the euils, the terrors, the calumnies, the enuies, the contentions, the dangers that men in such places must customarily meet with, that hee would much rather with alacritie haue posted on to his sepulcher, then to his greatnesse. *Brutus,* when hee determined his owne end, cried out with *Hercules, O wretched and miserable power of man! thou wert nothing but a name, yet I embraced thee as a glorious worke, but thou wert a bond-slave to fortune.*

It is superfluous to inlarge (or comment vpon) the sufferings of those famous men. Euery man's owne talent of wisdome, and share of tryall, may, with not much difficultie, conster the sence of their meanings. *A good man* is the man that euen the greatest or lowest should both *bee*, and resolue *to be ;* and this much may be confidently auerred, that men of eminent commands are not in generall more feared in the tyde of their greatnesse, then beloued in the ebbe of that greatnesse, if they beare it with moderation. Statists, honoured or fauoured, (for fauour and honour are for the most part inseparable) haue the eyes of the world vpon their carriage, in the carriage eyther of their glories or dejections. It is not to bee doubted (which is a singular comfort) but any sequestration from a woonted height is only but a tryall ; for beeing managed with humblenesse and gratitude, it may ennoble the patients (for their owne particulars) to demeane themselues excellently in the places they had before (may bee) somewhat too neglectfully discharged. Alwayes there is a rule in obseruation, positive and memorable, that an interposition, or ecclipse, of eminence must not so make

Plutarch in vit. Demost.

Dion. hist. Rom. lib. 47

a man vndervalue his owne desert, but that a *noble resolution* should still vphold its owne worth in deseruing well, if wee ayme, and intend, to repute and vse honours but as instrumental causes of vertuous effects in actions. To all such as so doe (and all should so doe that are worthy to bee such) a seruice not to be neglected is a proper debt, especially from inferiour ministers, to those whose creation hath not more giuen them the prerogatiues of *being men*, then the vertuous *resolution*, leading them by A LINE OF LIFE, hath adorned them with the just, knowne, and glorious titles of beeing *good men*.

VADUM *non transeat excors.*

FINIS.

NOTES.

Page 4, line 30. John Forde.] This is the mode in which the name is properly spelt, and not Ford, as it was sometimes printed, even by himself. John Forde's anagrammatic motto, prefixed to some of his later works, was *Fide Honor*, so that the final *e* in Forde is necessary to it.

Page 8, line 19. For their weak *ballac't* soules.] Here we have a direct authority for " ballast," instead of *ballasted* in " The Comedy of Errors," act iii., sc. 2 : it ought, of course, properly to be spelt " *ballac'd*."

Page 8, line 21. Needed a *redemption*.] In the original " redemption " is misprinted in the plural.

Page 8, line 25. Yes; it is doubtlessly *probable*.] " Probable " is here used in the sense of *proveable*.

Page 10, line 15. Doe I *conclude* true lovers.] The use of " conclude " for *include* was not uncommon ; and *vise versâ*. See " The Two Gentlemen of Verona," act v., sc. 4.

Page 12, line 1. To talke, converse, or *dallie*.] In the old copy " dallie " is misprinted *dailie*.

Page 16, line 18. Been *prest*.] i. e. ready, Fr. *prêt*. It occurs again in a poem near the end.

Page 19, line 6. Tamburlaine, the scourge of God.] It is evident, from his mode of spelling the names, as well as from what he says of Tamburlaine and Zenocrate, that Forde took his knowledge of them chiefly from Marlowe's drama of " Tamburlaine the Great," which was printed in 1590, and reprinted the year before " Honour Triumphant" came from the press.

Page 22, line 30. Was not Helen of Greece made a Trojan

stale ?]   " Stale," which usually means a bait, decoy, or pretence of some kind, is here used in rather a peculiar sense.

Page 24, line 28. Lucrece, the Roman dame.]   Forde seems to have had Shakespeare's poem in his mind when he wrote this passage.   T. Heywood's tragedy, " The Rape of Lucrece," was not printed until two years after this tract came from the press.

Page 36, line 1. Puissant is the Danish king, and strong.]   It was not usual at this date to employ " puissant " as a trisyllable : Shakespeare several times applies it as a dissyllable.

Page 37, line 31.

" Who are in nature false, yet free in name,
       Are servile slaves to feare, and fooles to shame."
These lines are marked as a quotation in the old copy; but it was frequently at that date a mode of noting passages which the author thought worthy of quotation, and not such as were quoted by himself from preceding writers.

Page 43, line 28. I *ingeniously* acknowledge.]   The words *ingenious* and *ingenuous*, now quite distinct in their meaning and application, were formerly confounded, and used almost indifferently : thus in " Timon of Athens," act ii., sc. 2, we have :—

——— " *ingeniously* I speak,
       No blame belongs to thee."
In " Love's Labours Lost," act i., sc. 2, in the question, " What! is an eel *ingenious ?*" the quarto, 1598, has it *ingenious*, and the folio, 1623, *ingenuous*.   Many other instances might be produced.

Page 44, line 22. And the presentor a *feodorie*.]   This is a word which occurs several times in Shakespeare, and it generally means an accomplice, or confederate : in " The Winter's Tale," act ii., sc. 1, we find " federary" in the old copies, but it is probably a misprint for feodary.   In " Cymbeline," act iii., sc. 2, Pisanio asks,—

——— " Senseless bauble,
       Art thou a *feodary* to this act ?"
It is in the sense of *confederate* that Forde employs it.

Page 46, line 17. The richest chain wherewith a good man can be adorned.]   Alluding, of course, to the custom of old, for persons of station to wear gold chains round their necks.

Page 49, line 25. The temperature of the mind followed the temperature of the body.] This axiom has been already inserted in the same words in "Honour Triumphant." See this vol., p. 21.

Page 50, line 29. In a *rushen* ring.] i. e. a ring of rushes, often used of old in sport, and sometimes in superstition.

Page 54, line 26. John, the last and yongest Lord Harrington.] This title is properly spelt Harington. John, " the last and youngest" who bore the title, came to it in 1613, and died in the following year, when the peerage became extinct. His father was John Lord Harington, created Baron Harington, of Exton, 21 July, 1603.

Page 55, line 16. For what man soever leaues.] It is deeply to be regretted that a page is here wanting in this character of Sir Walter Raleigh.

Page 57, line 10. To *becharme* their resolutions.] i. e. to *bewitch* or overcome their resolutions by a charm. The word occurs in Beaumont and Fletcher's " Laws of Candy."

Page 59, line 10. Women were in their creation ordained to be wooed and to be won.] See " Henry VI.," part i., act v., sc. 3.

" She's beautiful, and therefore to be wooed;

She is a woman, therefore to be won."

The last line is found in Robert Greene's " Planetomachia," quarto, 1585.

Page 60, line 22. As the beazar for his preservatives.] Alluding probably to the medicinal virtues formerly imputed to the *bezoar* stone.

Page 61, line 15. Charles Duke of Byron.] George Chapman wrote two fine dramas upon the life and fate of this French nobleman, which were first printed in 1608, and again in 1625.

Page 63, line 24. Learned [man] and philosopher.] The word *man* seems here accidentally to have dropped out in the press.

Page 63, line 29. Other *momentany* delights.] The words *momentany* and *momentary* were of old used somewhat indifferently. In " Midsummer Night's Dream," act i., sc. 1., "momentany " of the quarto editions in 1600 is printed *momentary* in the folio of 1623 (see Collier's note on the passage); but, nevertheless, "momentany" was used as late as the time of Dryden, so that we need not be surprised that Forde employed it in 1620.

Page 64, line 9. School-boyes, newly trayned up in the principles of grammar.] Alluding to the example in Lilly's Latin Grammar, then in use, *Vir bonus est quis*, &c.

Page 66, line 26. Like knights of the post.] See Nash's " Pierce Penniless's Supplication," 1592, (pp. 12 and 95 of the Shakespeare Society's reprint) for an explanation of the terms " knights of the post."

Page 67, line 23. Euen kings *and* private men.] Perhaps we ought to read " even kings *are* private men."

Page 68, line 22. To *surquedrie* in passions.] i. e. to *insolence* in passions : properly " surquedry" (an unusual word in prose, but often used in verse, especially by Spenser) means overweeningness, from *sur* and *cuider*, Fr., to think; so that it etymologically means insolence, or pride, arising out of too good an opinion of ourselves.

THE END.

LONDON:
F. SHOBERL, JUN, 51, RUPERT STREET, HAYMARKET,
PRINTER TO H. R. H. PRINCE ALBERT.